Paul Strube has been an educator in science and social science for over 30 years. He is a textbook author and currently the Senior Lecturer in Social Sciences for the Endeavour College of Natural Health in Adelaide, Australia. He has written scholarly and popular articles for a wide range of audiences and media, from radio to classrooms.

To my students, from whom I have received much more than I have given.

Paul Strube

PROPERTIES

Reflections from the Science Lab

AUSTIN MACAULEY PUBLISHERS™

LONDON · CAMBRIDGE · NEW YORK · SHARJAH

Ordering Information:
Quantity sales: special discounts are available on quantity purchases by corporations, associations, and others. For details, contact the publisher at the address below.

Publisher's Cataloging-in-Publication data
Strube, Paul
Properties: Reflections from the Science Lab

ISBN 9781643788036 (Paperback)
ISBN 9781643788029 (Hardback)
ISBN 9781645365235 (ePub e-book)

The main category of the book — EDUCATION / Essays

Library of Congress Control Number: 2019907955

www.austinmacauley.com/us

First Published (2019)
Austin Macauley Publishers LLC
40 Wall Street, 28th Floor
New York, NY 10005
USA

mail-usa@austinmacauley.com
+1 (646) 5125767

I would like to acknowledge the very kind and helpful support in the publication of this book given to me by the Endeavour College of Natural Health, based in Australia. Also, thanks to the *Australian Journal of Education in Chemistry*, in which the essay 'Porosity' first appeared, and is now used with permission. And, of course, the wonderful team at Austin Macauley for their support and guidance throughout this adventure.

Table of Contents

Foreword

These essays arose from a life-long interest in the relationships between science, education, and language. I have come to believe that, regardless of the powerful and important role of the school laboratory, and the newer digital technologies, the meaning and value of the concepts to be learned must inevitably be conveyed from one mind to another by language. It is there that the new is tied to the old. And most importantly, I believe that the surest way to tie that knot is through story. I have had the opportunity to see the power of story, used in its broadest sense, illuminate the understanding of countless students. Stories they were told, and stories they told in return.

For most of my professional career, I have been a teacher of the inanimate, of the roles that matter plays apart from its appearances in the living. I have found that the language we had to share as we wrestled with that inert world required us to tell stories about the fascinating and often unexpected ways in which the world of matter and the worlds of the learner and teacher intersected. It was those intersections that I hoped to explore in these essays.

Hardness

I

I have come to believe that, in spite of what the scientific journals report, any story of the interactions of matter and life cannot be told except as a modern fairy tale. And I believe this is so despite—or perhaps because of—the triumphs of modern science. We still know so little of either matter or life and are therefore liable to join them together in ways that the cyclotron bosses and the DNA masters should be more hesitant about.

That life is somehow compounded of matter and time, is certain; but there our confidence ends. Is life an inevitable consequence of matter in complex organization? Or has life seized on matter for purposes of its own? There has long been a religious tradition in the West that sees life as somehow entrapped within matter. The spirit is breathed into the inert clay, and the long struggle to return to an immaterial selfhood begins. Opposed to this is the view of life as a marvelous blending of matter, energy and time, the contemplation of which can provide insights into human nature and our sense of place and belonging.

For many years I have been a teacher of science, seeing the difficulties many students have with making connections between the sciences of matter and the sciences of life. Of course, by life they were thinking not about what it is or how it came into being, but about living things—the crazy, often absurd, amazing world of anteaters and toadstools and electric eels. It takes some time and patience to reach the point where they can appreciate the nature of the physical processes that underlie, indeed constitute, those various ways of making a living.

In most perspectives, matter has been seen as the more prosaic member of the partnership. Yet for something forever beyond direct human observation, it would have to be admitted that the atom, as the unit of matter and substrate of life, has come to be revealed as a fascinating object. Far more interesting at any rate than Newton made them sound when he described them, in part, as "...solid, massy, hard, impenetrable, moveable Particles..." Such an account conveys, as was probably intended, an image of little, dull steel pellets of various shapes, careering around in the vacuum. They hardly seemed likely constituents of the butterfly or the dandelion seed floating off into distant yet expected springs. No doubt Newton had quite specific ideas of what was meant by attributes such as 'massy' or 'hard,' and no doubt, too, that the smallest butterfly wing scale could be manufactured of such grit, if it be fine enough. Somewhere in the accretions of this dross, there arises the light step of the deer mouse, and the endless drift of great seaweeds under the sun. To understand such a transmutation, however, the mere existence of Newton's 'Particles' may not be enough.

Newton's views on anything should not, of course, be summed up in a single line. To complete his words on atoms, we must add "…and of such sizes and figures, and with such other properties, and in such proportion to Space, as most conducted to the End for which He formed them…" What are these 'other properties' that allow matter to meet the ends for which it was formed? In the time since Newton, scientists have uncovered some of the character traits of matter in the aggregate, traits which are still known as the properties of matter. The textbooks label them with surprisingly mellifluous terms: tenacity, malleability, porosity, and luster, for example. Are these the ill-assorted keys to an understanding of the entrapment of life in matter? Is it here that Newton's particles cross a threshold into the animate? In their enthusiasm for the success of the materialistic philosophy in physics, many 19th century biologists certainly thought so. Time has not yet realized their hopes. But science has, as a consequence of this search, revealed intricate interactions between matter and life of great power and fascination.

Many years ago, as a beginning teacher of science to young students, a glimpse of matter as the scaffolding of life was given to me. A short, black and white film was shown to the students on the process of cellular division. Though no details of intercellular structures could be seen, there was a clear sense of furious activity happening with the cellular membrane. The cytoplasm was trembling with the magnified tumult of its components; it seemed to be incredibly busy with life. The film ended with what, for me, was a moving, almost shocking scene of a cell dying. The cause was either unstated or long forgotten. But the cell came to an instant of pause, and then literally burst apart, spewing its contents in total chaos across the screen. It was as if that whole concerted frenzy of activity had not just underlain the life of the cell, but rather *was* that life; that effort and movement and molecular interplay somehow alone defined what we meant by cellular life. It was an image that, judging by the murmurs around the darkened classroom, carried a powerful, if uncertain message from the normally hidden underworld of life. For you see, it was clear that all that tumult of movement was being performed by structures and particles not themselves alive. The filaments and proteins and organelle membranes did not live, did not pulse with life; rather, they were instead the vibrancy on which life was built. It was a message, I see now, to do with the properties of matter, of the contribution of that far from inert clay to the conduct of living.

II

In the spirit, then, of a modern folk tale, consider the property of hardness.

Some of the oldest mountains in the world range along the southern border of Sinai. Ancient pre-Cambrian rocks lie exposed in a landscape noted for a harsh grandeur of climate and religion. Upon one of these mountains, Moses is said to have received the commandments of Jehovah on tablets of stone. In the marvelous scene from the Hollywood version of the story, Moses watches in awe and terror as God etches them with lightning into the stern granite of those hills. The powerful symbolism is made even more so by our realization that granite is one of the most enduring of materials, not easily weathered, and therefore ideal for eternal messages.

But being so hard, granite is not easily scratched; Moses on his own would have had a difficult task working such material with the soft metals of his day. It would be simpler to recast the story by eliminating granite for the impressionable tablets, and choosing soapstone instead. Long known to the ancient world, soapstone was frequently used for carving; Assyrian cylinder seals, Egyptian scarabs, and Chinese figurines were fashioned from this soft material. The presence of soapstone, or talc as it is also known, can be indirectly argued for by noting that it is a common product of metamorphism in igneous rock, especially olivine, which occurs in the adjoining Red Sea. At any rate, as the softest of minerals it would have been ideally suited to take the impressions of the Commandments, and there was a long precedent for such uses. Being so much lighter than granite, it would also help render more probable the account of Moses hurling the tablets at his wayward people (and thus washing his hands of them at the same time).

The difference in hardness between granite and talc was one of the difficult problems for early natural philosophy to explain, committed as they were to the idea that all matter was supposedly made from particles of equal hardness. It was quickly guessed that the answer would have to lie in the way the particles combine, but determining that underlying structure was the work of many years. It was first necessary to find out just what particles, and how many of each, composed the various substances; though answering that question often demanded the destruction of the structure of interest. But by the early 19th century, enough detail had been gathered to allow the new science of crystallography to pronounce with confidence on the nature of mineral hardness. And it did so through the work of one of the greatest scientists of that age.

Friedrich Mohs died in 1839 while on a journey to inspect the volcanic areas of Southern Italy. Fresh from intellectual triumph with the acceptance of his scale of hardness; from charges of plagiarism regarding his work on crystallography similar (perhaps too similar) to that of Weiss; from royal approbation with his appointment as Imperial Counsellor to the Exchequer in Vienna, he set off in late September for the Tirol region. His mind was filled with questions that his broad field experiences had prepared him to address. He knew of course that minerals differed significantly in their hardness, and he had first guessed, then proven, that this was due to their crystal symmetry. When broken apart, most minerals fall naturally into characteristic shapes, labelled with geometric precision; rhombohedral, pyramidal, orthorhombic, tesseral. His new challenge was to determine if, and how, these symmetry systems were determined by the way the mineral was formed. A rival idea placed the origins of symmetry in the constituents of the mineral; no matter how formed, the shapes of the atoms and the forces between them would combine to ensure the resulting regular pattern.

Mohs often worked alone, and even at the age of 66 could stride for hours along rugged outcrops, geologist's pick in hand and felt specimen bag slung around his waist. Thus it was only when he was several hours overdue from a routine inspection of local volcanic deposits that concern was expressed and a search begun. His body was found lying full stretch, with "...face composed and wearing an expression of mild surprise." Despite his vigor, the cause of death was put down to age, heart trouble, and the rigors of the plutonic landscape. It may be he was overcome by the escape of volcanic gases, not unlikely in that region, triggered perhaps by his hammer cracking the thin crust like an impatient parent eager to know the life within. The small collection of minerals found in the felt bag, soapstone among them, had often provided him with clues to the reality of events. In this final instance, they remained stubbornly mute.

In life, Mohs had often remarked on how miners scratched a rock with their fingernails to aid in determining its identity. The key was to see who scratched who. Many a miner's thumbnail bore the scored trails of feldspar and quartz; in return, gypsum bore the miner's signature. There is no evidence in the slender biographies of Mohs of similar mental scars, of whether his ideas of hardness were consciously shaped by the abrasions of his life. Like all of us, he bore the invisible scorings of his encounters with others. Like us, he must have brushed against those who are hardened, whether formed so or destined from birth. And he too may have known those whose softness has endangered their sustained existence, and who bear the impressed fingerprints of our clumsiness. Through the comparisons of such scorings, a scale by which to compare mineral hardness had been brought into geology. In the search for its underlying meanings, a man lay dead on the volcanic slopes of southern Italy. Science, more than most peaceful professions, can mark its growth in human lives.

I have often hesitated before the closed classroom door, and not always from simple nervousness. Over the years, it is possible to see the infinite variety of human character reveal itself in the struggle of these students to understand the complexities of matter as the sciences have revealed it. Every teacher has had the experience of seeing these encounters become, for some students, a trial of such emotional and psychological power that a whole life is transformed, sometimes in ways that are tragic. I recall an experience of a close colleague, charged with introducing beginning students to the fundamentals of biochemistry. She often expressed her concern over a young man, returning to study after an absence of several years, who was fiercely determined to succeed. He was, she feared, overcharged with an unalloyed conviction of his own powers of intellect. His interactions became one-dimensional, predicated solely on academic performance. We counseled, but were forced to watch helplessly as he narrowed his energies to one single plane of being, leaving all others exposed and vulnerable. An unforeseen failure on a critical piece of laboratory analysis led to a fatal shattering of personality, revealing the brittleness of the life he had built in defiance of the symmetry that gives even inanimate matter the strength to endure the abrasions of chance and flawed effort.

III

In the years following Mohs' death, the secret of mineral hardness was found to indeed be linked to his other great classification scheme, that of crystal symmetry. It would probably have delighted Newton to learn that, not his particles alone, but the arrangements of them in space, were responsible for the delicate flaking of talc. And it may have affirmed his religious ideas that those arrangements formed beautifully symmetrical patterns of geometrical starkness. Shape gives hardness, but in perhaps an unexpected way. Contrary to the classical view of the shapes of atoms as the explanation for the properties of matter in the aggregate, it is now seen that it is the pattern formed by the interplay of atomic forces between the atoms that establishes the causal foundations. The symmetrical balance of calcium, carbon, and oxygen in varying quantities, for example, is responsible for the multiple shapes of calcite (Hardness = 3, Moh's scale); prismatic Iceland spar, scalenohedral dogtooth spar, and plated argentine. And as calcium carbonate, these same atoms form the skeletons of myriads of invertebrates, who use a symmetry of their own to build shells of magnificent beauty. The shells are transformed into chalk, from the contemplation of which T.H. Huxley revealed the past history of life on our planet to a group of very rough diamonds (Hardness =10, Moh's scale) of the British working class in 1872, in his lecture "On a Piece of Chalk."

Diamond and graphite, both composed solely of carbon, yet dramatically different in hardness. The explanation seems to lie in the ability of the carbon atoms in diamond to form tetrahedrons; four-sided, triangular pyramids with each atom tied into place by four strong covalent bonds to neighboring atoms. By contrast, the carbon atoms of graphite bind in such a way as to form layered sheets which can slip easily past one another. In a similar fashion, those individuals with strength, with resilience to destructive shattering, may be those who, believing that all others are similar in their humanness to themselves, have formed firm bonds of love and compassion with all their neighbors. Their connections form in many directions, across cultures and times, between philosophies and diversities of ways of living. They are nowhere a stranger, except to prejudice. In nature, diamonds are formed when carbon is placed under great pressure and high temperatures, transforming coal into jeweled flame. The idea of resilience in human beings too is often the result of such social and personal pressures, though it may instead lead to an unfortunate shattering. For more commonly, our lives show the planes of weakness that reveal our stubborn bigotries and petty hatreds, marring the crystal and preventing it from igniting into splendor. Or a whole society becomes stratified into layers that only weakly connect to each other, so movement is along one plane only. Like graphite under the miner's thumbnail, such cultures may be more easily scored by history.

IV

The measurement of hardness today is far more sophisticated than a single stroke of a fingernail. Samples whose hardness is to be determined are pressed with a diamond or steel 'indenter'; the ratio of the size of the resulting impression to the magnitude of the applied force gives a Knoop's number within the range of 1 for pitch to 8500 for diamond. The testing is precise and elaborate, with special care taken with materials that are normally very brittle, such as glass. It is intriguing to learn that one of the strongest recommendations for the Knoop number procedure comes from the fact that its results agree remarkably well with those of Mohs, developed over 125 years prior. Among the results to emerge from this work has been the dependence of hardness on direction—some materials are harder when pushed, say, from side to side than when squeezed from top to bottom. Again this appears to be due to symmetry, and is familiar in the analogous idea of the strength of wood against and with the grain. Here, the symmetry is strongly affected by the way the substance, whether wood or mineral or human, grows.

The materialist, concerned to find a clue to the secret of life, will not be completely disappointed in a study of mineral hardness. The long preparation of technique and analysis that has gone into the understanding of crystal structure led indirectly to our unraveling of the arrangement of the atoms within DNA. Here we find not an inert strength but a beautiful example of an organization open to chance and change while still enforcing a basic structure that has seemingly persisted for billions of years. On a coarser scale, the hardness of mineral bone and teeth has found some elucidation through the work of the mineralogists.

But it is not within the arrangements of atoms and the balancing of forces into delicate symmetries that matter slips over into life. That these are necessary powers of matter is incontestable; life is dependent on structure. Yet we know that numerous and highly complex molecular organizations often result only in unyielding crystals, utterly lacking that intense activity we associate with the living. Indeed, life can be defined through its ability to use the order of the crystal for its own ends, rejecting its limitations while building on its strengths.

The property of hardness has a deeper role to play in the understanding of life through its analogies with human experience. Though gifted with a certain native hardness by the genetic accidents of birth, the very process of living develops within us a grain, lines of weakness or strength that come to be us, that come to be seen by others as part of the symmetry of our being. We become hardened to the forces of fate and human blundering, as some still molten facet of our personality freezes into rigidity. Under the pressing weight of love and compassion, however, some icy crystal of thought or belief may slowly regain a measure of warm response. And we still count experience by marking who has left their deepest impressions, for good or ill, on our thoughts and acts.

Conductivity

**The mind is not a vessel to be filled,
but a fire to be kindled.**

Plutarch

I

If there is one thing human beings are extremely good at, it is causing change. We are, it seems, surprisingly dissatisfied with conditions as we find them. We want things to happen, and novel things most of all. The American philosopher Santayana made the point that "change is odious to the animal, whose existence is bound to certainty." And it may also be true that our restlessness is confined mainly to Western civilization. The surviving remnants of tribal human groups seem to have contented themselves with a more static order of existence, built on cyclical or mythical conceptions. However expressed, it seems clear that animals have an ethology and some of us, at any rate, have history, and as far back as the records go we've been busy having lots of it.

Change is dependent on difference; a perfectly homogeneous universe or society would be timeless, or to say the same thing, changeless. In our case, however, rich and complex variety is characteristic of the world we

24

inhabit, and when any one of us gets wind of any aspect of such diversity, change is possible. Somehow, word gets around that things aren't the same over there; their gods are different, their children seldom laugh, they build with stone. It is the sort of news that carries change within it, as the winds carry seed and spore. In the past, the news was carried from place to place by travelers, wandering under the influence of some private restlessness. Filled with their own personal energy, they arrived in new places to release creative vigor in the form of stories, song, art, and the artefacts of living. Now, trade and caravan routes and modern flight paths have become the convection currents of change. Today, more than ever before, we can all feel the wind of it on our faces.

Such change may be random, the currents being indifferent to the flotsam they carry. Purposeful, directed change, on the other hand, is the business of education, carefully reshaping the individual's life by providing access to the stored understandings of the culture. The passage of ideas or experience through the generations resembles, in an uncanny way, the passage of heat or electricity through material substances. In considering electrical conductivity, for example, we can see how, as in education, the task is to encourage the spark in the right direction.

II

Some time ago, the *Sciences* magazine carried a short account by H.C. von Baeyer of the physicists' quest for access to high voltages. He told in passing a tragic story. In 1928, a German scientist named Kurt Urban fell to his death while attempting to adjust apparatus for gathering the intense electrical energy of lightning. He and his team had strung a 610-meter cable across a gorge on Mount Generoso in Switzerland to capture the furious energy of the lightning spark and successfully recorded an electric potential of 8 million volts. Drawn to the mountainous region by a personal restless curiosity, Urban found a violent death, not at the hands of the lightning he came to tame but in the remorseless yet far weaker grip of gravity.

To complete their experiments, Urban needed an electrical conductor. Though we're not given this detail in the story, it is most probable that copper was used, as its conductivity is greater than that of any other metal except silver. There is just the possibility, however, that Urban used aluminum, which was first used as an overhead conductor in Switzerland. Reinforced by a central core of galvanized steel wire, these aluminum based conductors spanned great distances without appreciable sag. But whether copper or aluminum, the explanation for excellence in conducting electricity lies at the atomic level. In the words of the electrical engineers, "In metals, the conduction of current is a role of the free electrons exclusively. When a voltage difference is applied to a metallic specimen, the negatively charged electrons are attracted to the more positive end of the metal. This flow of electronic charge is what we measure as electric current."

Copper's 'free electrons' are those which, as in all metals, are only loosely bound to the central nucleus. The atomic structure of the individual copper atom, combined with the crystalline structure formed when large numbers of them join together in a length of copper wire, ensures the presence of these lightly held electrons in sufficient number for the purpose of conduction. The 'passage' of electricity through a copper wire thus depends crucially on both the freedom and the basic similarity of these electrons.

Similarly, in the process of educational conductivity, the passage of culture across the generations demands the freedom and continuity of a people in space, time, number, and language. This is true whether we mean the education of the young by the tribe or through the formal institutions established in the modern world. History has repeatedly told of the destruction of a culture as the dispersals and decimations of war or plague break the generations' long links with the past; social anthropologists point out how the loss of a native language necessarily means the loss of crucial articulations of meaning. By contrast, in an intact society, the teacher is the temporary repository for the valued, essential intellectual and creative resources of the community. Society structures itself so that, under the influence of the mediators of tradition or change, the young are initiated into the meaningful life of the people.

In the copper wire, the applied voltage difference allows the metallic specimen to be instantly saturated with an electric field. Every charged particle immediately feels the influence, and those free to do so begin to move in response. Random motion becomes directed movement, in response to some changing factor in the outside world. Educationally, this voltage difference represents the internal, driving force of tradition and the external connections of the society to the dynamo of the outside world. In times of isolation and peace, the voltage is low, steady, slowly drawing the young from childhood to the full potential of mature participation in the society. The teacher's task is then to prepare their charges for known roles, for traditional wisdoms. In times of rapid social change, when the voltage is 'high,' when unrest and uncertainty about whether the nature of the future is in fact known, education itself often undergoes complex changes when stability would serve it and its culture, best. Raising the temperature of a metallic conductor lowers its electrical conductivity; the motion of the free electrons is too violently perturbed by the rapid vibrational motions of the separate atoms. Conversely, near perfect conduction is achieved by bringing the metal close to the absolute zero of temperature. Within the classroom, as every teacher knows, a calm working temperature, full of the natural vibrational energy of people engaged in meaningful tasks without hurry, provides optimal conditions for the currents of purposeful change.

III

The conduction of the vibrational energy of heat through solids is, on a theoretical level, not as clearly elucidated as for electricity. In simplest terms, the heat energy is transferred because the accelerated vibration of atoms at the heated end sets adjoining particles vibrating through contact, a process that continues until every atom shares in the increased motion. In contrast to electrical conductivity, no equivalent heat 'field' is established in the metal; atoms must wait for the vibration to arrive. The process is thus much slower and crucially dependent on close connections between neighboring atoms.

Silver is the metal with the highest thermal conductivity. This ability to conduct vibrational energy assures us, for example, that a 15 cm long silver spoon, in a cup of boiling water, will transfer about 10kcal of heat to our tentative fingers per minute, until the spoon itself grows too hot to touch. Increasing the temperature of the spoon does not significantly interfere with the process, but the rate of transfer does depend on the temperature difference between its two ends.

It turns out to be true that most good conductors of electricity are also good conductors of heat. Why this should be so may not be easy to see until the role of the free electrons is given closer examination. Acquiring high vibrational or kinetic energy at the heated end, these electrons can speed past many atoms before colliding with a distant atom and sharing with it their higher energy. They act in a sense as the advance guard or forewarners of the coming change. In any society, there have been personalities and events of great cultural power and meaning for the members of that society. When the system of education is whole and intact, the resonances from those crucial moments can travel freely until all members share in them. Perhaps it might be said that the culture now exists in a state of higher intellectual or social energy. The teacher may in fact be the first resonator to such historical or innovative ideas that the young encounter. Human acts vibrate with potentiality. We still resonate to messages from the past, to those human gestures that transcend culture, that make us less inarticulate, that reaffirm. In a society with traditions of educational coherence, these human acts will more easily find receptive minds both within and outside the classroom. In other words, a society itself can be said to have an 'educational conductivity' directly related to the structure of that society and the value it places on education.

The extreme opposite of conductivity is represented by the insulator, a natural or crafted material that resists the conduction of electricity or heat. Of course, the best insulator is in fact nothing at all, the vacuum. Self-confident, vital societies look with compassion and pity at the moral and conceptual vacuum to which the mentally ill are often condemned, while attempting to eliminate conditions which insulate their members from the varied richness of experience.

The analogy is rendered more complicated, yet perhaps more complete, by the additional factor of purpose. Rapidity of conduction, whether of electricity, heat, or ideas, is neither desirable nor detrimental in its own right but becomes so only when the purpose has been decided on. And it is here I believe that education is receiving confused guidance from a society unsure of its directions. When what it means to be a human being is uncertain, education cannot meaningfully prepare the young by initiating them into mature participation. Students and their teachers tend to resonate to every available energy, meaningless change repeatedly sweeps through the society, the increased vibrations remaining unharnessed and potentially destructive. At such times, society may be best served by teachers seeking to conduct in classrooms only those resonances of proven worth and ennoblement, those transcultural human acts that assert humane purposes to life.

IV

As a professional educator, I have heard and participated in the perennial debates on education. In essence, there are only two questions; what should a mature, fully participatory human being be like and what is worth knowing? The second, of course, can only be answered if the first has been decided upon, but too often the answer to the former is assumed. In the area of science education, for example, answers to both questions tend to revolve around discussions of the nature of science itself. Is science a method, a way of knowing, or is it a collection of facts, theories, and experimental protocols? Is it 'process' or 'product?' In terms of the metaphors being explored here, what should the conductor be connected to; the data or the method? To what purpose is the conductor to be put? What dynamo shall power it, and what engine will it serve?

T.H. Huxley wrote a textbook for science students, first published in 1880 and entitled *Introductory*. In it he gives his now well-known definition of science.

"...Science is perfected common sense. Scientific reasoning is simply very careful common reasoning, and common knowledge grows into scientific knowledge as it becomes more and more exact and complete. The way to science lies through common knowledge; we must extend that knowledge by careful observation and experiment, and thus arrive at rational explanations of natural phenomena, which may suffice for our guidance in life."

Perhaps this is only 19th century science and naïve. Perhaps it only represents a man and a time of great confidence and optimism. But many science teachers spend their limited energies in helping to prepare an adult population who can act as Huxley urges. In a profession filled with caring, often over-burdened men and women, it is wonderful to see the respect and joy that animates them at the memory of those students, that handful among many, who so succeed. They are the ones for whom teaching becomes the experience of putting them in true contact with greater, rarer minds and works. And the teacher's only selfish reward is seeing, as Plutarch states, the mind of another kindled into flame "for our guidance in life."

It is doubtful that such students will ever be more than a minority. The vagaries of nature and society will continue to allot us to mediocrity or greatness in due measure. But education can, in the society that values it highly, begin to unlock the potentialities only fully realizable in adulthood. It no longer allows the responsible adult to say 'I didn't know any better.' It takes away excuses for ignorant action and forces the individual to act on and be known by ethical and moral principles. It therefore provides not only the tools for continued learning and skills in 'perfected common sense'; it provides exposure to the great ethical, social, and intellectual thinkers of our history.

There is a further dimension to these ideas. Education is often said to ideally serve the ends of life. In a time when the ends of life seem to be narrowed to a grasping obsession with money and image, such a role for education would be terrible to contemplate. Educators must take responsibility for shaping human purposes in line with the greatness of the ideas they are charged to transmit. In this sense, science education is as well placed as any of the traditional disciplines. Both its method and its subject are rich with possibility. Science is fortunate to have such fascinating, mysterious objects for our attention as quarks, snowstorms, and rainforests. And we've been here such a short time, we've hardly gotten to know the place at all. Science continually reveals the myriad complexity of the simplest elements of our home. It has given some of us the reality and all of us the opportunity to participate as discoverers of the nature of ourselves and our home. And to do this it has made a necessity of truth to fact, honesty of statement, respect for endeavor, and patience with error.

More specifically, though I admit it's a prejudiced opinion, I would urge the teaching of the sciences of Matter. The unraveling of the secrets of this obdurate, infinitely varied, and supremely useful material has provided us with intellectual and aesthetic achievements of great subtlety and power. As the carrier of life and consciousness, as the substratum of art, as the constituents of our planetary and cosmic home, it serves all purposes well. To understand it, to shape it, to take delight in it—these are abilities and traits the gaining of which would demand the firmest connections to the finest minds and accomplishments of our history.

Density

I

"In all areas of thought," wrote Medawar, himself a master of expository prose, "which science or philosophy can lay claim to, including those upon which literature has also a proper claim, no one who has something original or important to say will willingly run the risk of being misunderstood; people who write obscurely are either unskilled in writing or up to mischief."

There is of course a great deal of truth in this. As an example of the 'mischief' Medawar refers to, we have Robert Hookes' famous anagram designed to establish intellectual priority for his discovery of the relation between the force applied to a spring and the distance it stretches. And as an example of obscure writing, there is the unfortunate Thomas Young, whose prose was so unwieldy that the British Admiralty reluctantly refused his no-doubt valuable advice on stresses in ships' timbers because they simply couldn't understand a word of it.

The example of Hookes is perhaps easier to account for, given the human desire for recognition and fame. Today, our prize and patent hungry scientists simply keep quiet until they can establish priority in print. Young's case is far more interesting. Genius of course may often be misunderstood, but that is more commonly due to the revolutionary nature of the ideas presented, rather than the quality of their exposition. And in science, at any rate, there is a tradition of a writing style which insists on unambiguous clarity, a tradition that should have come to Young's aid in his communications with the Admiralty. What is this tradition, and what has it to do with density?

Well, take a pycnometer. The name alone is rich with those transformations from Greek to English that seem to so delight the linguist. *Puknos* means 'thick' and has undergone linguistic mutation into pyknic and hence pyncno; a pycnometer measures 'thickness' or density. (References to the pycnometer for use in *intellectual* testing, however, do not seem to have entered the literature of educational psychology as yet.) They are most familiar under their other name of hydrometers, used in measuring the density of the contents of our car batteries and home wine and beer brewing experiments. The instructions accompanying these store-bought pycnometers do not inform us of the underlying theory of their use. They simply indicate the correct way to drop it into the vat and the consequences, for the ultimate consumer, of its flotation at any given level. Even the thickest among us can use them to measure densities to a very high degree of accuracy. But how do they work?

A glance at the standard texts immediately immerses us in the traditional prose of the scientific paper. Even the family encyclopedia can't seem to resist this style:

Of the pycnometers in use for measuring the densities of liquids, one of the simplest consists of a glass tube of about 10 cc capacity, to which has been sealed a length of about 4cm of 0.5mm bore capillary. After cleansing successively with chromic acid, nitric acid, hot water, absolute alcohol, and dry acetone; the vessel, supported by wire, is weighed empty, full of water, and finally full of the liquid being examined.

In terms of the information contained per sentence and the amount of background knowledge assumed, they are, in a linguistic sense, extremely dense.

Before looking more closely at the origins of such a prose style, it is necessary to say something about the *purpose* of the above passage. It is written to inform a reader about a procedure; it is not attempting an explanation of that procedure (i.e. why it works) or why any part of the procedure is necessary. In short, it's a description. And there seems no intrinsic reason why a description needs to be couched in the prose style of a scientific paper. Classroom teachers, for example, have a wide variety of stylistic techniques for conveying information—including scientific information—clearly and interestingly without resorting to such a dense style. Why should it be necessary to become skilled at reading such prose to gain an understanding of how to use my pycnometer or indeed of how it works? Part of the answer to that question is involved in the study of genre or styles of writing and speaking.

II

By the time of Cicero, it had become customary to define the character of the three officially recognized genera by reference to the effect of each upon the audience. The *genus humile* was best adapted to teaching or telling its hearers something; the *genus medium* delighted them or gave them pleasure; and the *genus grande* roused them and excited them to action. Our concern here is with the genus humile, or common style, which became known in the 17th century as the Attic style. Aristotle had long before given its three essential characteristics as clearness, brevity, and appropriateness. Clearness, though itself often defined ambiguously, was best seen through contrast with its opposite, deliberate darkness. Hooke's anagram, for example, negated clearness. As Aristotle put it, clearness referred to the attempt to "...depict the effort of the athletic and disciplined mind in its progress toward the unattainable goal of ultimate knowledge." As such, it was meant to elucidate the nature of the enquiry as well as its results and findings.

Brevity is almost always assumed to mean saying a lot in only a few words, a meaning that leads directly to the dense prose of the encyclopedia. But for Aristotle and the rhetoricians of the 17th century, brevity was "...a quality that is almost necessarily involved in the attempt to portray exactly the immediate motions of the mind." What is shed are all features felt to be superfluous to the intended meaning. There is no mention of the need to condense thought into smaller packages, the main result of which is increased abstraction rather than clarity or ease of understanding. Instead, the "long musical periods of public discourse" are to be broken up into short, incisive sentences, each of stronger, sharper emphasis. This brevity was felt to be suited to private, personal communication as opposed to public, formal expression.

Aristotle's views on appropriateness were interpreted to mean that the style should suit both the audience and the subject; it should be neither too lofty nor too mean. Appropriateness to audience, however, meant more than just not talking down to the masses. It was instead, in the words of the old rhetoricians: A style appropriate to the mind of the speaker, one that portrays the process of acquiring the truth rather than the secure possession of it and expresses ideas not only with clearness and brevity but also with the ardor in which they were first conceived.

Unfortunately, later rhetoricians altered the idea of appropriateness away from both the audience *and* subject, toward that of audience *or* subject. This change led directly to the scientific style, in which the author and reader could be safely ignored in favor of the subject. Jacob Bronowski once quoted T.S. Eliot as saying, "There is nothing more important for a civilization than the invention of a new literary style." Here we see that argument in reverse. A great literary style has been torn apart, separating the listener from the content, the moving human effort from the thing found.

Particularly sad is the loss of interest in the genus humile by writers of merit and lovers of language. The chief characteristics of the style originally were figures of wit and an abundance of metaphor, which Aristotle referred to as "...the greatest of the figures by which literature may interpret the exact realities of experience." Surprising as it may now seem, clarity and brevity were once felt to reside within metaphor, which in turn was the key element of the language of teaching and description. For the modern writer, literature has come to exclude non-fictional writing and the province of metaphor, that great device for 'interpreting the exact realities of experience,' belongs solely to the poet and novelist. In large measure this has been due to the actions of the scientists themselves, who seized on the new distinction between audience and subject matter for their own ends. In 1666, the newly formed Royal Society in Britain soundly criticized the use of figurative language in reports to that august body, endorsing instead a 'mathematical plainness' that has been the tradition ever since. In an effort to impose objectivity on the reports of its members by rejecting "the painted scenes and pageants of the brain," they encouraged the process of converting wit into density.

III

The impact of all this has been profound and its consequences for learning about or taking an interest in science have been generally unexplored. To return to the amateur wine-makers' interest in their pycnometer for a moment, consider what happens if they want to know what density actually is, rather than how it is measured. If there happens to be an old physics textbook lying around the house, chances are that what will be given is a definition of density as the ratio of mass to volume, followed by a table of characteristic values. Textbooks have traditionally been very good at providing definitions but ignoring explanations, which is one reason most people know *what* things are but not *why* they are. Somehow the idea has arisen that giving something a label is equivalent to understanding it. In this sense, it certainly is not clear why gold, for example, of density 19.3 units, has the edge over concrete, a mere 2.3 units. Is the explanation to be found in bigger atoms or heavier molecules? Or is it better packing? Perhaps it is here that metaphor can be most helpful.

Interestingly, the more common understanding of density as crowded or packed in comes closer to a physical interpretation for the values in the textbook's tables. It seems to be a question of how close together the atoms can get. To arrive at that understanding, however, the intrepid home brewer would have to wade through a great deal more technical prose of a very reader-unfriendly type. The crystallographers have done most of the work here too, determining the geometric arrays of atoms within solids. For liquids, the ideas have been modified by what is known as the 'hole theory.' Fluidity is not just, as you might expect, defined simply as the ability of the substance to take the form of the confining vessel. Rather, in accordance with true scientific insistence on density of expression, it is the inability of the substance to support a static shear force. You can't divide up a glass of water with a knife, and it is the purpose of the hole theory to tell you why not. The alcohols in the wine vats, in which are floating those pycnometers of all shapes and sizes, appear to have the same types of crystal structure as solid, frozen alcohols, but with 'holes' where roughly each 12th atom should be. It is these holes which give liquids their fluidity. It's an engaging simple idea; to change that solidly packed crowd into a flowing stream, provide an exit for every 12th person. Instead of being surrounded by 12 neighbors, each crowd member has, on the average, 11 people, and one vacant hole surrounding them. There's always somewhere to sidestep to, and resistance to static shear force drops to zero.

The same principle of packing applies to the density of gold versus, say, aluminum. The component parts of both metals; the protons, neutrons, and electrons are all the same; all protons, for instance, are believed to be exactly alike. Ignoring the insignificantly massive electrons, gold has 197 protons and neutrons in its nucleus, aluminum has 27. Yet both atoms have the same radius and therefore volume. With 7 times as many particles in the same space, gold registers a density over 7 times that of aluminum. This is in stunning analogy to the whole notion of stylistic brevity as it has become; in both cases, packing more into equal volumes increases the density.

The difference in density between water and alcohol is not so well explained. Both are molecules, not elements, and our current knowledge of liquid structure is far less complete than for solids or gases. The simplistic answer seems to be that, while alcohol molecules have greater mass than those of water, they don't pack together nearly as well. The pycnometers bobbing around under the expectant scrutiny of the oenologists and brewers is especially sensitive to the looseness of this packing. Under the influence of the buoyancy conditions so dramatically uncovered by Archimedes, their own untidily arranged molecules delicately probe the three-dimensional network of occupied and unoccupied spaces in the depths of the vat.

Unable to exert a static shear, they sink until a density balance is struck between their own structure and that of the fluid. The denser the liquid, the less it sinks.

IV

Turning back to language, what does it mean to call technical prose unfriendly? To quote Medawar again, it might be better to think of it as "...very advanced, very grown-up, something we learn to appreciate, not something that comes to us naturally." And this is true, of course; as with all things of worth, appreciation only comes with sensitive effort. For the purposes of communicating between experts, it is perhaps absolutely unavoidable. But there are other aspects of this language that raise interesting speculations about its effects on the users. For example, science has come to make the distinction between the imaginative, creative act of discovery and the impersonal, precise account of what is discovered. Unfortunately, the accounts of the former are rarely published. As a result, the human heart of science is seldom revealed to outsiders. The classic story of Archimedes' discovery of the principle of density is one of the few in literature and still makes a delightful story.

Also, the reality of the scientific process is left unstated, leaving the impression of startling, unexpected breakthroughs popping out under the hands of researchers after a few days of tinkering with apparatus. The mundane work at the bench or in the library; the painstaking efforts to get the equipment to work properly (which may mean to give you the answers you expect); the hours of statistical and error analysis; the interplay of theory, observation, and wishful thinking; all are unexplored.

The enquiring mind seeks to penetrate the depths of natural phenomena. One way to do so is as the active researcher, forced to use native 'density' in the search for clarity. Another is through reading about the methods and results of those researchers. If the density of the prose is too great, even the sharpest intellect will be incapable of piercing the surface. The reader should encounter some 'holes' in the prose, filled not with 'Mathematical plainness,' but the story of the active, vigoros mind in its encounters with the world. This may be out of place in a specialist scientific paper but it is urgently needed in the communications from the laboratory bench to the kitchen table, where the human pycnometers struggle with the density of scientific prose.

Luster

The imperfect is our paradise.
Note that, in this bitterness, delight,
Since the imperfect is so hot in us,
Lies in flawed words and stubborn sounds.

Wallace Stevens

I

At some unknowable point in our transition from primate to human, it appears that a Stranger (perhaps a Visitor only) took up residence in our uncertain hearts. Called variously the Divine, the Oversoul, the Transcendent, its presence has called forth the wavering, often-eclipsed feelings of love and pity that distinguish the human act. In many cultures, its symbol has been Light, of purity and radiant softness, powerfully conveying its tender strength.

Though often portrayed in the religious painting of European art, such light is only fleetingly glimpsed in the everyday world. The perceptive yet skeptical mind is often hesitant to acknowledge its presence even if willing to concede its possibility. As a teacher of science, I have a personal and professional conviction of the power of symbols to achieve a hold on the human mind and imagination; a hold strong enough to call forth and embody their presence in the mundane. And, I now believe, when one works consciously with the interactions of light and matter, some hint of their true symbolic power is perhaps more likely to occur. I have little doubt, therefore, that my own experiences are neither unique nor exceptional. But whenever a glimpse of mystery is allowed, we are called upon to record it, however hesitantly, as a message from the intangible night of nature. Like the great radio telescopes listening to the rustle of hydrogen between the stars, we are tuned to subtle messages.

II

A common difficulty in teaching the young about the nature of light arises when questions of perception enter the discussion. Once the idea that objects can only be seen by emitting or reflecting light is made clear, if often follows that students come to ask if what they are seeing is the object at all, or are they only seeing light itself. Further difficulties arise when they also admit that a light ray can travel unperceived through the air; that light is, in short, invisible, yet gives visibility to everything else.

The working hours of a teacher, away from the rigidities of the timetable, are erratic, only tenuously linked to the school bell. In this instance, I had remained behind in the classroom rather late in the evening to finish preparations for an optics demonstration the following morning. A beam of light from a small point source was to be bent and dispersed through a series of lenses, revealing the property of refraction in classic textbook form. I was slightly dissatisfied with the procedure, however. The images cast on the screen were focused and clear, but the pathways of the light beam themselves were, of course, invisible, and remembering my students' difficulties with this idea, I was anxious to find a convincing remedy. (These are things they don't teach you in teacher training.)

Now the tried and true solution to this problem is to sprinkle a handful of fine chalk dust into the path of the beam. You can get a feel for how long ago this was because I then dutifully collected a small amount from the chalk ledge and, turning out the lights to enhance the effect, lightly flung the powder between the lenses. Immediately, a gleaming, splendid snowstorm burst into existence, swirling through the diameter of the beam and defining its presence by their lambent twinkle. I watched entranced, noticing as never before the slow, gentle tumbling of the grains through the softened white light; how each one cast its tiny shadow and reflected the momentary brilliance onto nearby specks.

Out of darkness into fleeting brilliance, I thought, transformed by light. Again and again I tossed the powder, with a growing certainty that my perception had been granted some fortuitous twist. Worlds, tumbling through the radiance of distant stars must gleam so, I mused, though this vision did not hold me long. "The world was created," said a man struck blind by his own visions, "by the word of God so that what is seen is made out of things that do not appear." Though he might have been speaking of the soul ignited by the grace of his God, the words echoed in my mind as these humbler particles shone and drifted.

There was, I knew, a more objective explanation of the interaction of light and matter that produced this silent sparking. Through a powerful leap of vision, the human mind has come to know of the incredible hail of ghostly photons on the equally insubstantial molecular surface of the chalk granules. This fleeting quantum association is responsible for all the optical properties of matter. Substances such as chalk give what is termed a 'dull or earthy' luster due to their opacity and the fact that their irregular, roughened surfaces scatter incoming light in all directions. Such 'diffuse reflection,' intones one authority, "occurs when the average depth of the surface irregularities of the reflector is greater than the wavelength of the incident light." Usually, a significant amount of light is also absorbed; white chalk is somewhat exceptional in this regard, though even its brightness is subdued.

Both visions are important for understanding more of nature and of humankind. In urging the mind toward the infinitesimal, we uncover the magnificence of matter. And in the sensitive reading of such transient phenomena, we glimpse the divine. The words of St. Paul, regardless of our religious affiliations, are those of a man searching deeply for insights into the essence of that Stranger who points always above and beyond our flawed human nature. In doing so, he shared an insight that modern science, in its own experimental way, has brought within the understanding of all and confirmed. T.H. Huxley once gave a lecture titled "On a Piece of Chalk" to the working men of 19th century England. He had summoned up for them the sound of huge seas surging onto primeval beaches where the shells that formed the chalk once lived. Perhaps wisely, he did not further touch on its possibilities for invoking what I hesitatingly named to myself the sacred. Through long experience with students, I would refrain also, hoping that the sight of the flashing grains would create its own hints in the minds of some observers. The harsh light of the classroom drowned out the scintillating particles as I finished my preparations for the morning; the chalk dust on my sleeves was once again a common powder. But I had seen my vision, and now the chalk would not only whisper of the long story of life's struggle in distant waters but something of the light that reveals the Stranger's presence in the human act of understanding.

III

Chalk is a brittle thing to hang much learning on. Over the years of countless students and the demands of a challenging profession, it becomes easier to see such tenuous encounters as beguiling tricks of an inconstant nature, without force or meaning. One becomes more proficient, it is true, but there are times when a growing cynicism is seen to conceal an emptiness not always filled by attention to duties. That, however, is a common story. In my own case, at least, I found that I retained a special respect for the optics bench; a manipulator of light and glass that occasionally revealed, as Bacon put it, nature "caught undisguised."

For example, a usual classroom exercise is to allow the students to explore the property of refraction by passing light rays through triangular glass prisms. In this case, the bending of the ray, rather than its separation into its constituent colors, was the intended effect; the prism's surfaces were roughened, and one only saw the beam enter, then emerge in a different direction.

Or so I thought. In the darkened room, the students bent over their apparatus, I overheard one young girl exclaim to her partner, "Look, it's filled up with light!" Glancing over her shoulder, I saw the prism glowing softly from its multiple internal reflections. Triggered by the girl's words, my mind's eye was momentarily cleared to witness what, in truth, I had merely seen many times before. The glass, through which light normally passed cleanly suffering only an angled twist, was now shining as if filled with a rich, luminous fluid. Trapped in a three-walled hall of mirrors, the light rays were confined by some critical angle to what was now a glass prison. What was transparent was now translucent, the crizzled surfaces causing infinite scattering of the beam. Here was the luster known as vitreous, that of broken glass, characteristic of substances with a refractive index of around 1.5 and the most common in the mineral kingdom. Such might have been the words I used to answer their questions, but we all sensed, I think, that such answers did not touch on the full meaning of that lucent prism.

It was only later, while doubtfully searching through old textbooks for the laws of such translucence, that I realized something of the true significance of what we had seen. Built of common earth, roughened by the misfortunes and checks of life, our usual response is only to deflect the light that shines within. But at times, especially in the nobility of the compassionate act, we twist ourselves through some critical angle that ignites us into a kind of luminosity. There is no need for this light to shine for others to see, though it has done so enough in the past for it to be known. And if we do not always shine, then there is some comfort in knowing that it is our very imperfections that make it possible.

I have come to be ever more impressed by the way the humble elements of earth can be fired to a soft brilliance. Knowing that the interactions of light and matter are of such transient impalpability makes it all the more astounding. In each of us there is the possibility of refracting the divine through the flawed materials of the human self. Chalk and glass—the shells of ancient creatures and the sands of the beaches on which they lived—have drawn hopeful messages with the rays from the optics bench.

IV

It is no surprise that my cautious visions had come to me in a professional way, so to speak. I was beginning to know matter in the way the materials scientist knows it, though I was coming to suspect it had properties not normally considered in the standard texts. In terms of the old debates about the separation of matter from spirit, or soul from flesh, I increasingly wondered if matter might not be, in some unguessable way, the rough, durable cloak of spirit.

I was to have one more such professional courtesy granted to me, at a time when I had left teaching to complete a higher degree. Freed from the task of interpreting matter to others, I felt less wary of considering its subtler impacts on my own thinking. Just as the early atomic researchers saw the solar system mirrored in the atom, I was finding that the messages written into even the commonest substance conveyed something of the restless, ambiguous nature of humankind.

An invitation to attend a demonstration of new instruments for the teaching of optics came my way. It coincided with a much-needed break from study, and colleagues from earlier institutions would be there. Part of its appeal, too, lay in the fact that a historical overview of the development of lasers would be included; lasers were quite unfamiliar to me, and it seemed, so my teaching voice said, opportune. For the most part it was the usual thing: expert salespeople, expensive brochures, and the technology of modern science teaching. I wandered off into the dimly lit area set aside for the laser display, dutifully reading the explanatory cards and peering into the silent models. As my eye swept over the exhibit, it was easy to see the normal technical progression from large and clumsy to small and simple; the gradual increase in power and versatility and the increased pace of modification. To me, technical change has always seemed characteristic of us as a species. It's something we are very good at, and given time and resources our artefacts always conform so beautifully to hand and eye and task.

One smaller display finally drew my attention; an uncut ruby crystal, about 15 cm long and 2 cm thick. Next to it lay the polished cylinder into which it would be shaped, the outside ground to a fine frostiness, the ends completely transparent. I was pleased to read that the near-perfect parallelism of the two ends had been achieved using an optics bench; each was flat to within one-quarter of the wavelength of sodium light. The exhibitors had arranged that by pressing a button, light would pulse through both crystal and cylinder—more for aesthetics than function, I imagined.

The rich brilliance of the ruby light was startling, casting deep shadows and overwhelming the diffuse light in the rest of the room. Its glow was that of stained glass in old cathedrals but even more pellucid in its immediacy and strength. It was so clear and cold that I shivered, faintly sensing its strength from a distant region of energy and power, indifferent to what it illuminated. The light of the inanimate, unsoftened by the needs and wishes of life, was pouring into the room. It was unstained.

Much later, I discovered that such effulgence is referred to as adamantine luster, due to a high refractive index. These crystals had been slowly cooled from the unutterable chaos of the molten state. Their cold gleaming hinted of the times their atoms had known of the inferno of interstellar storms, of the wastes of the arctic winter; a nature not inclined to be kind to life and perhaps with purposes of its own. The coldest eye of science could only draw the most reluctant analogies under that pure gleaming. Science is never at its best when faced with what used to be known as the ideal, with the essence of light and matter. For a few moments, I had been allowed to experience both. There were no messages here for us, this was no attempt by the Stranger to guide or hint. Here was only matter, only light, both revealed through a necessary and beautiful blending. It was with a proud arrogance that we sought to know and master these entities, I thought then, bathed in that adamantine light. They will lie forever remote, far and high above our grasp, composing the very instruments we use to study them.

V

"We carry with us the wonders we seek without us," said Thomas Browne in a 17th century text. He was celebrating a re-awakening of the dignity and glory of the human being. Though Browne was undoubtedly referring to the religious sense peculiar to man, his words can be given additional meaning through the context of their time. The contrast between the Medieval and Renaissance view of the body and matter generally, is a familiar one. By 1642, the world of matter was under thoughtful investigation, both by natural philosophers and explorers of oceans and new lands. It was indeed a time of wonders.

In all such revolutions of thought, something is lost and something gained. Light was no longer suffused with the properties of the divine, though it was to retain a rich allegoric power. Subjected to the relentless analysis of the new sciences, it proved, however, to be even more complex and fascinating than its mythic history had suggested. In making it part of the natural world, we forfeited some of its symbolic value, but gained a rich, though still incomplete, intellectual mastery. Through the technical skills of the crafts, light would bend its way through microscope and telescope, vastly extending our grasp of the material world. It was a blending of light and matter that would hurl society into a future beyond the imaginings of the 17th century.

The experiences with light that I have recounted convinced me of the richness of an understanding informed by science. Yet I knew how impoverished the scientific view was on its own; indeed, how it could easily lead to a facile disregard of the wondrous. At the opening of his poem *Evening Without Angels,* Wallace Stevens quotes two lines from Mario Rossi: "the great interests of man; air and light, the joy of having a body, the voluptuousness of looking." The poet takes up these themes:

"Light too, encrusts us making visible

The motions of the mind and giving form

To moodiest nothings…"

I had seen the chalk dust gleaming, the prism fill with light, and the ruby flame. In each case, the poet's words were true, and the motions of the mind set into new, perhaps warmer orbit. Professionally, it was hard to resist thinking of the Stranger as a teacher, engaged in providing experiences that suggest the infinite rather than confine to present knowledge. But it was not until much later, when all these episodes were desiccating in the back pages of memory like pinned butterflies in forgotten museum drawers that something of the true nature of the Visitor was shown to me.

This time it had, at least outwardly, nothing to do with science or teaching. A rare collection of Egyptian artefacts was temporarily on display at the local museum. I have never been a serious student of the past, but an increasing respect for the craftsmanship of early civilizations provided the incentive. I was, to be honest, tired of the black boxes of modern technology. Antique scientific instruments seemed to more closely mirror the relationship between science, technology, and human skill that delighted me. No such instruments would come from the tombs of the Pharaohs, I knew; they employed the shipbuilders' art to sail to God. What I hoped to see were the magnificent artefacts crafted to accompany them.

The collection was arranged as found in the Pharaoh's burial chamber; the lighting came from small but intense concealed spotlights. It was not too difficult to imagine your way back over 4000 years, waiting as the dead god-king was being slowly carried to this room. What sounds would have been heard here, I wondered. Would it have been the grieving voices of women, or the skilled court musicians performing a final quiet hymn to the departed god? Such a vigorous people may have farewelled their ruler with a triumphant riot of music, eulogy, and dance. Little would have carried to this small room at the heart of the pyramid, but perhaps the whispers of the waiting priests would have echoed, whispers that concealed their own doubts and longings. In that other room, the torchlight would have flickered over the gleaming gems and bright paintings, the wrought statues, and kingly furnishings from the royal household.

Here the relics dazzled the eye under the harsher light of our age. Small placards asked us not to touch the crafted vessels whose very outline invited the hand to clasp and rejoice. The eye was asked, in the very "…voluptuousness of looking," to do the job of hand as well. There were few manufactured materials here, but mainly elementals—pottery clay, gemstones, and the metals—brass, bronze, copper, silver, gold. The artisans had taken the given matter of the earth and coaxed it into the artefact. In almost every instance, they had chosen to finish their work by altering the way its surface interacted with light. They had polished and painted and glazed items that were kept in total darkness for over 4 millennia. Under what strange sun did they foresee these objects shining?

The centerpiece of the exhibit was a full-sized gold death mask. It was that of a young woman, the first bride of the king, who had died in childbirth. The brief notice accompanying the mask hinted that, in remembrance of his love, the grieving king had ensured that she too would have a place in the celestial boat. The curators had departed from their theme by displaying it set upright on a tall pedestal draped in burgundy cloth, separately illuminated. It was a triumph of the goldsmith's art; one wonders if their fingers trembled under the anxious eyes of the young Pharaoh. If flesh could be alchemically turned to gold, just so would it look. It shone under the light in that rare manner peculiar to gold alone; rich, lustrous, warm. Time had left it untarnished, the very symbol of death conquered.

And here for me was the human act raised to that rare perfection which stills all doubt, whose presence is peace. Love and grief had seized the elements of matter and made of them a passionate, defiant symbol to cross millennia. The presence of the Stranger was there; in the love of the mineral-rich Earth, the love of the artisans for the gold under their skillful touch, the delight in the play of light on surfaces, in the poignant, familiar love of one for another. It enters the heart with a bliss compounded of our own joys and tears; we smile at their imagined tender moments, know too the bitter pain of his loss. If there is anything of greatness in us, I thought then, it must lie here, in a love given an ages-leaping voice through the joy of joining light and matter.

VI

It may be that, in the incremental advances of the human nervous system, something like what I have termed the Stranger becomes inevitable. That it should take the form of feelings of transcendence through compassion, may fall within the reach of evolutionary biology. I am very open minded on the topic of the powers inherent in matter and do not need to see it merely as the mute servant of something greater.

Not long ago, I listened to a technical expert's lecture on the subject of modern day prospecting for ore. He made much of the use of new scanning electron microscope studies of tiny, one-celled organisms which concentrate the metals and reveal their presence. Only in passing did he refer to luster as an identifiable property of minerals. Afterward, I had pulled out my old lecture notes to reacquaint myself with the robust vocabulary of luster classification; metallic, adamantine, vitreous, resinous, greasy, pearly, silky, and dull or earthy. Some the poets have conjured with; others are workmanlike, still useful. In each is hidden a specific scientific meaning that refers to structure and its effects on impinging light.

And hidden in each too is a story; in chalk, glass, ruby, and gold. I think now the human story is told in this way too, of the structure of a life and how it shines in the near darkness.

"Let this be clear that we are men of sun

And men of clay and never of pointed night…" states the poet and he asks, "Was the sun concoct for angels or for men?" Study the gold mask, which love had crafted to mingle with the sun. Both its visage and its making are our own.

Porosity

**Being an extract from the reminisces of the late
Elwood K. Flinton, Ph.D.**

I

Of course it's the popular thing in modern science to laugh at the ancient alchemists; especially that polite sort of laughter that reminds you so strongly of assured intellectual superiority. But never forget that those guys were the originators of some very original ideas. Nowadays, we tend to accept the fact that they had important skills for developing certain techniques and bits of apparatus, while lambasting their mystical, pseudo-scientific theories. In retrospect, to the man with an open mind, some of those old-fashioned notions had just enough of a kernel of truth, or plain common sense, to lead to something valuable.

My own work, for example, got a nudge in the right direction by reading about the alchemists' desire to find or make the alkahest, the perfect solvent. Think of it, a liquid in which everything will dissolve! That's a pretty bold idea for those so-called mystics! It immediately appealed to me, for several strong reasons. First, I liked the idea of chemists getting their hands on a perfect anything. For too long, in my view, the physicists have had all the running here, with their 'perfectly elastic mediums' and 'perfectly reflective surfaces.' Why should chemistry be constantly relegated to an empirically impure reality? It would be neat to have been able to reduce the hundred-odd elements down to one perfect atom, but there you are, we're stuck with the damned things, I know that. So naturally I was attracted to the vision behind the search for a perfect solvent. Furthermore, it wouldn't be a hypothetical construct like those physicists use, of course—it would actually exist, the real thing. There would be a Nobel in that for sure, and the commercial spinoffs would be phenomenal.

Not that I set out to find it myself, of course. No, for that task I knew I was both too dumb and too smart. Too dumb in that I hadn't kept up with all the latest quantum chemistry where the answer, if possible, would have to be found. A job for a younger man, I'm afraid; though with a large enough grant I could have set up a team and led them there. I must admit I hesitated over that for a while, but the thought of trying to get such a proposal approved by those stodgy, tight-fisted funding bodies made me weep. A total lack of vision, those guys. And that's the point I reached when it occurred to me that I was too smart to undertake the job. You know why? Because by God, if anyone else ever did make the alkahest, then one thing they were going to have a great deal—a very great deal—of trouble with was something to put it in. A perfect solvent would just dissolve any container you tried—glass, metal, plastic, whatever. So how are you going to keep it? Let me tell you, I lost some sleep over that one. Everything I thought of, I was forced to reject. For example, keeping it frozen *might* solve some of the storage problems, but when it came time to thaw it out and use the stuff, then what? Any substance you wanted dissolved would end up contaminated with bits of container.

There was a theoretical problem too, that I don't mind telling you I've never solved and which still gives me nightmares. A perfect solvent, of course, dissolves any substance. But, does it also dissolve any *amount* of substance? Would a perfect solvent dissolve an *infinite amount* of something? If that was true, if that was part of it being perfect, one drop of the alkahest, splashed on the floor, would dissolve the entire Earth! To make a long story short, my deep fears about the consequences of a leak in any vessel containing the alkahest led me to the task of designing the perfectly non-porous container—the Flinton bottle.

As you may know, I was, in at least one sense, well prepared for such a job. My background in physical chemistry gave me certain skills in the analysis of the properties of substances, of course, and more specifically my own field of powder chemistry made me familiar with some of the peculiarities of porous surfaces. Down in the ultra-structure of a layer of clay dust, for example, there's about as much empty space between the grains as there is solid matter. Water and air have little problem moving through. In fact, almost everything we know is full of holes, and making something water or air proof is no simple task; just ask an engineer. Sometimes, I felt that what we call solid matter is nothing more than empty space stitched together with fine cotton.

Now, I'm a methodical worker, so I went back to basics. Even though it was obvious my bottle couldn't be made of anything material, I knew it was important to find out how impermeability had been solved by others. I had a Ph.D. student named Wallace who was ideal for this job. First of all, of course, he was cheap; I had no grant for this, remember. Secondly, he had already been working for months on another idea of mine which I'd picked from the alchemists—an antidote for the Elixir of Life, if one was ever found. Wallace was clearly in the field, as it were. To be honest, Wallace was almost totally helpless if you put him in front of a burette and compelled him to titrate anything. No technique, no feel for the apparatus. What he could do though, was the non-glamorous, unrecognized, but essential part of scientific research. That boy could do literature searches like a demon. He knew the journals, the offprints, the databases; he could run the computer searches and the microfiche readers. He could pull every reference, however obscure, out of the Dewey Decimal system like God pulling muons out of the vacuum. He threw light into dark places—the back issues of scientific journals. I suppose it sounds like I'm getting carried away, but that's where scientific research really begins; who's done what already, how, and with what results. Until you know that, you're either re-inventing the wheel or having a long look at a lot of blind alleys.

So Wallace digs up a mountain of stuff about holes in pottery and the science of glazing; about holes in wood and the art of sealants; about holes in metals and the folklore of galvanizing; and holes in membranes and the usual biologists' ignorance about guard cells, active transport, and reverse osmosis. It appeared that no matter what substance you looked at, there were going to be holes. I had to revise my definition of solid matter, too; it now read, wherever the holes aren't.

But how did you deal with them? Well, sometimes you capped them with something you hoped had smaller or fewer holes, like the top of a saltshaker. Or you filled them in, like glue in cracks, substituting little adhesive holes for large gaping holes. Sometimes you tried bending the hole right around, so that as fast as anything entered it from one side, it leaked right back in through the other; heating sometimes did that to ceramics. And if you were really clever, you put a little living guard cell on each hole to shut it off when something tried creeping through, like a cat outside a mouse hole.

We looked at what causes holes in the first place, down at the molecular level, that is. Weeks were spent studying cubic closest packing and hexagonal arrays; the whole geometrical language of the crystallographers who worry about how atoms pack together. No matter how you squeezed them in, there was always some space between the damned things. And it wasn't just a technical problem. Atoms weren't allowed to get too cozy—the Pauli Exclusion Principle wouldn't permit it. Wallace pointed out that we'd have to go for a container made from the surface of a neutron star for really small holes; but a cubic centimeter of that stuff weighs about 100 tons. And where do you get it, anyway?

Before rejecting a material Flinton bottle as completely out of the question, it occurred to me that I could do it—just—if some way could be found of keeping the alkahest from actually touching its sides. A cushion of air, for example, between bottle and liquid, though of course air wouldn't work as, no matter how much I pumped in, it would be rapidly dissolved. We toyed with the idea of separating the two with an electromagnetic field. We could make the alkahest positively charged, for example, by dissolving some positive iron ions in it, then make the bottle positive as well, and let them repel each other. It sounded promising but didn't come to anything after all. Too unstable; the slightest sloshing and the damned thing short circuits.

There was no escaping it; we had to go for something non-material. Wallace emerged from the depths of a particularly grueling computer search with the discouraging news that the physicists had the lead on this one. They had been working on a 'magnetic bottle' to contain the intensely hot plasma that results from their nuclear fusion experiments. It wasn't a true bottle, but a spherical magnetic field in space—a force field, if you like. I don't mind telling you that at first I didn't like it at all. Fooling around with some physicists' hi-tech contraption to solve an alchemical problem seemed all wrong. But I had to admit it sounded feasible. After all, a magnetic field, or at least a *perfect* magnetic field, should be seamless, completely whole. And being immaterial, it couldn't rust or corrode, spilling alkahest everywhere. As the stuff was being made, the manufacturer only need toss in a handful of some suitable diamagnetic substance such as bismuth. Building one, and making it portable as a Dewar flask, seemed mere technical problems.

Well, it should have worked, if only because it was such a neat idea. But as the great T.H. Huxley once said, there's nothing sadder than a beautiful theory destroyed by an ugly fact. It turned out that my magnetic field Flinton bottle was full of holes, with an ugly fact sitting in each one of them. First of all, it turned out that a magnetic field is not nice and holeless after all. Being a field, it shares in the lumpy nature of all quantum physics; it comes in bits. Secondly, the supposed vacuum surrounding the alkahest isn't even close to being empty. It's a crazy realm of virtual particles and exchange photons, popping in and out of existence in billionth's of a twinkling, ripe for dissolving in the alkahest. And finally, the ugliest fact of all, the one that forced Wallace and me to give it up at last and turn to something else. It turns out that the alkahest could get through even if there weren't any holes at all! They could employ what's known as 'quantum tunneling' and pop through the walls without the slightest need for a hole. That's the sort of thing the Uncertainty Principle lets you get away with.

A real shame, of course. But as Wallace pointed out at the time, even if it had been possible, it would have only been as safe as your power supply. The Flinton Generator, the commercial spinoffs of which have funded my early retirement, was originally conceived to meet such a need. If the alkahest is ever a reality, perhaps I'll be acknowledged as having played some part in its success.

Plasticity

I

The human love of stories is one of the happier gifts of a random evolution. We are, it seems, compulsive storytellers, making them up as we go along, writing them down, enchanting ourselves. But sometimes we are told a story by nature and find it as wonderful as those our poets conceive. We listen happily, astoundedly, to stories of dinosaurs or thunderstorms, or that smaller, nervous spark at the origin of thought. If your taste runs to epics, the Earth itself has many long stories to tell. There are those that speak of events that happened a long time ago; the origin of the oceans, the thousand-year long winters of the Ice Ages, or the fiery birth of the planet itself. And there are those stories still being told, still unfolding; the movements of the continents over the mantle, or the mighty legend of the daily weather.

At the heart of all these stories, I believe, is matter, whether inert or taken up into the dynamism of the living. Even our most spiritual longings carry the taint of entrapment within a material body and our visions are bounded, however loosely, by the limits of sensory perception. Conscious life is the great story of matter

66

seeking to know itself, its possibilities, and its purposes. In the words of Emerson, "What is man but nature's finer success in self-explications?" To know itself, nature tells us stories, which we have been in the habit of reading since we first were human. Our readings are always hesitant, uncertain; the meanings changing with the passing of generations. But out of these readings the human story itself is woven.

The desire to understand and use matter is at the heart of our most valued human activities. For example, there is the deep, hard-won knowledge of soil by the farmer, wind by the sailor, or clay by the potter. The musician is intimate with sound, the painter with pigment, the dancer with the tension of muscle. Of all these, the scientist probes deeper into the constituents of substance, enriching our knowledge of long-familiar materials and providing us with many new ones, ripe for exploration by the creative. Yet in the scientists' sensitive, highly skilled analysis of the atom and molecule, the delight that can be taken in the sensuous, sometimes brutal, sometimes intimate aspects of matter is often lost. The story is often read, too often read, as a pallid record of fact, though there is no necessity for such a reading. Indeed, some have seen matter as but one of the many faces of God.

Between the views of the scientist and craftsperson, though closer to the latter than is generally recognized, there is that of the engineer or technician. For them, as for the artist, matter is pragmatic, obdurate stuff to be shaped to the human will. It is hammered, ground, torched, bent, and melted into submission; though it is always a partial surrender, the victories short. In one crucial respect, however, the creative artists and craftsmen differ markedly from the technician. The ideal of the engineers is standardized, uniform materials; flawless, homogeneous, well behaved. In both the production and treatment of engineered goods, there is an obsession with standards. And while both seek to unlock the potentialities inherent in the materials, the engineer has the task of extracting and shaping pure, standardized samples of known properties. It is an unremitting, highly complex effort that reveals the character of the technician as well as that of the substance. It is a story well worth telling, for in these interactions something of the nature of human thought can be glimpsed.

II

Others besides scientists have spoken with natural wonder of the complex, chartless, uncertain realm of life that has arisen from a material world, seemingly bound rigidly to laws of great beauty and simplicity. And there is no doubt that the behavior of carbon, for example, is far simpler and more predictable than that of the most primitive cell. But the gap between them should not be too quickly exaggerated; matter itself can act in ways far removed from the inflexibility often assigned to it. In order to see the plasticity of matter's adherence even to the laws of mechanics, consider beryllium, the fourth element in the Periodic Table. A lightweight, steel-gray, sweet tasting metal, it tells, in the words of the materials scientists, a good, clean story.

Beryllium is estimated to occur in the world's igneous rocks to the extent of only 0.006%, mainly as the ore beryl.

Extraction of the pure metal is a superb example of modern metallurgical art and is worth detailing at some length. In the words of the technician's manual:

"...beryl ore is fused at 1,500–1,600°C and then quenched with water to produce a reactive glass or frit. This material is heat treated to increase its reactivity, ground to a fine powder, mixed and heated with an excess of concentrated sulphuric acid, leached with water, and from the resulting solution of beryllium and aluminum sulphates, the bulk of the aluminum is separated as crystalized ammonium alum..."

Further steps are necessary to convert to pure metal.

I like to read passages of this kind to my students when we first begin our study of matter. I do so because I want them to understand that, if we want beryllium, if we want to use this substance for human purposes, then we are going to have to do some serious hard work. Gone are the days when we hoped to control matter by magic or force of will. Nature is only commanded, as the scientists know, by obeying her. We have to learn to read her stories aright.

When finished with, beryllium can be expected to arrive in the materials testing lab with a very high purity, well over 99%. There it is subjected to a series of tests to determine its suitability for manufacturing purposes. Beryllium performs well under such pressure. It shows a high melting point (1,285°C), excellent electrical conductivity, high heat absorption, and good mechanical properties at high temperatures. The next step shows the exacting demands placed on both the engineer and the metal. A final test piece is carefully machined to an exactly specified size. Often it's a cylinder, wider at the ends than in the middle, 5 ± 0.002

cm long, and an end diameter in the permissible range from 8.000–8.005 cm. The ± sign signifies the range of error the machinist is willing to admit to, otherwise known as the tolerance. The allowable limits of tolerance are set by the national or international authorities responsible for standards. The careful preparation of a substance for its planned destruction is, admittedly, one activity shared by technologists and munitions manufacturers. But there the similarity ends; one is concerned with the setting of standards, the other with their denial.

The testing machine may be an Izod impact-testing machine, manufactured by the Tinius Olsen Testing Machine Company. Securely bolted to the floor, it represents several thousand dollars' worth of computerized engineering whose sole job is to strike the beryllium test piece a shattering blow. Or it may be a tensiometer, designed to pull the test piece violently apart. In that case, the beryllium shows what is referred to as a very high modulus of elasticity. And it's here that uncertainties begin, and the carefully extracted and prepared beryllium starts to show its individuality and disdain for the laws of matter. This part of the story goes back to the early days of the 19th century.

In 1807, Thomas Young first expressed the results of his research into the behavior of substances when pulled or compressed. In what has been called a "model of cumbersome obscurity," he phrased them thus:

"We may express the elasticity of any substance which may be denominated the modulus of its elasticity, and of which the weight is such that any addition to it would increase it in the same proportion as the weight added would shorten, by its pressure, a portion of substance of equal diameter."

Even in Young's day this needed decoding. The force (usually a pulling force as in our tensiometer) applied to the test piece was seen to change its length (or degree of twist) in a uniform way. The ratio of the applied force to the change in length is still referred to as Young's Modulus and identifies each material specifically enough for tables of moduli to be published. But if you look up the entry for beryllium, there is evidence of immediate qualification. First of all, the modulus depends crucially on metallic grain size, purity of content, and directionality—like wood, it's stronger in some directions than others. Secondly, beryllium obviously loses all rigidity if molten, so temperature must be specified. For the comfort of the engineer, room temperature is usually agreed on, but modulus values at different temperatures are also given. Therefore, the Young's modulus for beryllium ranges from 15–100 units.

The behavior of the metal shows these complications clearly. The beryllium test piece (at a specified temperature) is clamped into the tensiometer and stretched. And at first all goes well. As the force increases, the beryllium lengthens by just the amount promised by the published modulus. Furthermore, in these early stages, if the force is reduced to zero, the beryllium returns to its original shape; that is, it behaves as an elastic solid. But as the force steadily increases toward a point known as the *elastic limit*, two things immediately become apparent. The change in length no longer follows the modulus value. Instead, it elongates at an alarming rate. Secondly, when the force is removed, the test piece no longer has the ability to recover its original shape. It is permanently deformed as its atoms are inexorably pulled away from each other and for a short time it behaves like soft clay. Increasing the force still further continues to distort the beryllium until the elastic limit is exceeded and the sample snaps, often destructively shattering.

The measurement of the forces and temperatures specific to the destruction of beryllium are well ahead of the theoretical understanding of what is in fact happening inside the test piece. The laws of physical science have not yet reached, even in the imagination, into the complexity at the heart of beryllium. The gap between theory and practice is so large that engineers routinely build in large safety factors when designing structures containing beryllium. The pragmatic knowledge of the engineer, hard won as it is, lacks definitive explanation.

III

The engineer looks with respectful mistrust at the materials that pass through the destructive testing machines. Where is the hidden flaw, the unseen unconformity, that will disastrously lower the elastic limit and hurl the proud structure to ruin? With even greater, perhaps anguished mistrust, the compassionate observer of modern society searches the lives that pass in the street. There are no pure test pieces, none of us come refined from the crucible as a measure of all others. Marred, misshaped by the hammer blows of genetics and environment, we deny the engineers' needs. Yet in crucial ways this plasticity, this refusal to meet engineered standards, defines our humanity. Under the ordinary stress of life, for example, we have great resilience; our elastic limit is set very high. If we ask what in fact sets or defines our elastic limit, we see that the metaphor goes much deeper and involves the stories we tell each other, our shared lives. Linguists and literary scholars have often commented on the powerful, indeed essential 'plasticity' of human language. Under the pressure of change, of the forces imposed on life by the tensiometer of experience, words take on altered meanings. And like wax impressed with a thumbprint, they can assume the meaning and identity of the users. By doing so, they enable us not only to cope with change but to actively create understandings. This is seen by some, in fact, as the defining characteristic of the human species. Our lack of social and linguistic rigidity allows the fullest range of possibilities to be explored or at least endured.

But all too frequently the stresses approach closely or pass beyond the human elastic limit, beyond what even language and pity can manage to contend with. With beryllium and all metals, the resulting behavior is characterized by the terms malleability and ductility. A malleable metal responds plastically to forces of compression. Gold and lead are classic examples; gold can be beaten into sheets only 0.001 cm thick; lead can be pressed by the metalsmith into countless shapes. And the word malleable provides the sociologist with a ready analogy for human conformity. Under the steady external pressures imposed by society, most of us to some degree take the shape of our fellows in custom, belief, and action. The atomic units of either metal or society move compliantly into place. The result gives coherence and uniformity which in turn allows, perhaps surprisingly, adaptability to a wide range of possible structures. Coherent, uniform societies take many forms; tribal, democratic, totalitarian, theocratic. The one denied to them is anarchic. If the pressures become too great, however, or too prolonged, the individual's unique personality may be beaten to transparent thinness, ultimately to shatter.

A further defining character of any malleable substance is a lack of strength under tensional or pulling forces. They resist being separated from their fellows, preferring a communal existence to the tenuousness of the thread. As a societal characteristic, such extreme conformity raises images of the faceless totalitarian state, where the value placed on the individual has been extinguished in favor of a uniform common person. It is here we see the sharp edge of our metaphor. In the metals, we can assume the strict, indeed ultimate, identity of the atoms that compose it. Such identity would be intolerable in a healthy society, where the conformity must be leavened both by desirable human variety and free human choice.

The ductile metals behave very differently. They are readily drawn into fine strands, like copper or platinum. External tensions pull them into a desperate, tenuous coherence to the extent where tenacity is not only a measure of the breaking strength in wire but a recognized human character. Perhaps that is part of the reason why the most tenacious materials known are products of living things— the spider's web, the sheep's wool. Weight for weight, they are many times the strength of steel.

The ductiles are not always malleable as well. Antimony, a highly ductile metal, immediately shatters when subjected to the forces of compression. In this it resembles those among us who, though easily destroyed by the conformist pressures of society, are somehow drawn into higher, more creative realms, communicating to us through their tenuous yet strong links with our common humanity. Yet they too can be pulled into madness, into spaces so remote no messages can arrive through the frayed wires.

Beryllium lacks ductility but has other properties which put it in demand by those who build the atomic furnaces, whether for peace or war. And there are other metals such as zinc which lack both malleability and ductility and are therefore brittle. Zinc, however, when alloyed with copper forms bronze, which has given us the name of a whole period in human history. There are parallels with the individuals in our society unfortunate enough to lack almost all resistance to the pressures of life. Their shattering comes easily and early. Perhaps there is hope for them, if they become alloyed with friendship, compassion, and love.

The shattering of beryllium test pieces is done in the name of standards. The similar destruction of priceless human lives is the commonly perceived tragedy of mental illness, delinquency, and despair. We speak cautiously of knowing our limits, of feeling for that thin line over which plastic deformation becomes social and spiritual deformity. Even before such extreme limits are reached, the individual may suffer great unhappiness. After concluding his work on elasticity, Young was asked to undertake another great work concerned with standards, this time of length. The

British government, concerned over the unwieldy definition of meter used at that time, wished Young to find a more convenient measure. While engaged in this task, he continued to work on what he is perhaps best known for, the decipherment of the Rosetta Stone. In this he was the rival of Champollion, who according to some accounts built on the unacknowledged work of Young to complete the decipherment in triumph. In this long, painstaking effort to unlock the voices of a vanished civilization, Young found there were no standards by which to judge jealous rivalry, the swaying of public acclaim, or the true measure of greatness. The dispute left him bitter and unhappy, a victim perhaps of his unfortunate writing style as much as of his rivals.

IV

The engineer, like the craft worker, is content with the knowledge of materials gained through pragmatic experience, but the scientist seeks an explanation at a deeper level, as does the philosopher, and spiritual leader. For all three, explanations are to be found only in worlds remote from common sensory experience. Malleability and ductility demand recourse to that invisible, atomic world of potent energies and bizarre entities. And though this ultimate explanation may lie on the intangible bedrock of the quantum, some glimpse is also given through a study of the structure of the metal; that is, how the atoms are arranged in space. The powerful effect of shape is seen to determine much of the behavior of the material. Beryllium is described by the crystallographers as displaying 'hexagonal closest packing.' The atoms are arranged around a hexagonal framework in such a way that they resist movement in all directions but one. A more ductile metal, such as iron, moves easily in all directions due to its 'cubic closest packing' arrangement. In effect, beryllium contains a plane of weakness, unavoidably built into the heart of the crystal by the inflexible forces of atomic bonding. Yet this very weakness makes beryllium more resistant to the human will, more difficult to shape and flow to our demands. The shattering of brittle personalities is stark evidence of the tragic resistance to conformity that can occur when the plane of weakness lies close to the heart and mind. And the thought and culture of a whole people can contain just such a flaw, its inflexible social views and prejudices creating confusion and turmoil, to be broken under the hammer blows of history.

If the planes of weakness were all that influenced the plasticity of metals, the engineer's task would be greatly simplified. Theory and experience would combine to predict the behavior of shaped materials with great accuracy. For example, the barrier between elastic deformation (return to shape) and plastic deformation (permanently changed) would be more easily determined. But the complexity of substance only begins with crystal structure. Purity is of at least equal importance. This must be seen in two ways, as purity of atomic arrangement and purity of composition.

In the first, every crystal of beryllium is seen to be flawed in structure; atoms are missing, there are gaps or excesses in the number and position of constituents. These flaws are known to the engineer as dislocations and they are responsible for the disconcerting ease with which materials fracture and distort. Pervasive, unpredictable, they are never totally eliminated, creeping through the metal like crystalline ghosts. These flaws arise during the vagaries of crystal growth. And like our own maturity, the beryllium crystal shows the effects of an environment full of chance and change.

The other impurity is that of composition, as foreign atoms intrude into the crystal's lattice. These contaminants can drastically change the properties of the metal, sometimes in ways eagerly sought by the engineer as alloys. As we have seen with zinc, much of the story of the human triumph has been the mastery of alloys; such as bronze, brass, and steel. And there is also that more elusive alloying of matter and life, life and mind, mind and spirit. In the ages-long struggle with the materials of both the inanimate world and the creative human imagination, we have gained a mastery that would have astonished our early ancestors. The limits of physical law, far from shackling the powers inherent in matter, have only highlighted the superb organizing power of the mind. Loren Eiseley talked of both kinds of power when he wrote:

> But still
> No one knows surely why
> Specific crystals meet
> In a specific order.
> Therefore we grasp
> Two things:
> That rarely
> Two slightly different substances will grow

Even together
But the one added ingredient
Will transfigure
A colorless transparency
To midnight blue
Or build the ruby's fire.
Further, we know
That if one grows a crystal
It should lie
Under the spell of its own fluid
Be kept in a cool canyon
Remote from any violence or
Intrusion from the dust.
So we
Our wide men in their wildernesses
Have sought
To charm to similar translucence
The cloudy crystal of the mind.

Here in the words of the poet, the storyteller, we see the greatness inherent in the plasticity of human language and creative gifts. Without the benefits of standardized materials or the technology of the engineer, he shapes the most elusive substance of all into structures of abiding beauty and meaning. And in this act, in this great gift of story, we find the counter to the despair of our flawed nature.

Shape

I

On the occasion of the 1886 celebrations of his 50 years as Professor of Natural Philosophy at Glasgow, Lord Kelvin spoke candidly of his professional career. "One word characterizes the most strenuous of the efforts for the advancement of science that I have made perseveringly during fifty-five years; that word is failure." After admitting his continued ignorance of the grand ideas of the physics of his day, he added rather poignantly, "something of sadness must come of failure."

One of those great ideas whose final elucidation eluded even the finest minds of the previous century was the structure and composition of what Kelvin termed 'ponderable matter.' The varying atomic theories were united behind the idea that the properties of matter in the aggregate, as evident to the unaided senses, were the consequences of atomic properties. "The extension, hardness, impenetrability, mobility, and force of inertia of the whole arises from the extension, hardness, etc. of the parts..." wrote Newton in 1713, adding "and this is the foundation of the whole of philosophy."

Now there is both a logic and a danger in this transfer of the macrocosm to the infinitesimal. The logic was sufficient to satisfy generations of physical scientists in their search for understanding. Even today, we still weave the large-scale features of the world from atoms having the far more intangible properties of charm, strangeness, and spin. The danger is one that may occur to the student of life before impinging on the mathematical genius of a Newton. For life is a characteristic of matter evident to the senses and it would be a daring act of imagination to assign life to the very atoms. Nonetheless, the immediate task before the scientists of the 19th century was to continue Newton's program for natural philosophy and account in detail for the properties of the whole in terms of its parts.

For example, matter is of course 'ponderable' in Kelvin's sense; we can be brought up short against it at any moment. To explain this on the atomic scale, two rival views long battled for acceptance. One saw the units of matter as mathematical points, like those of the geometer. The rigidity of matter was due to their being centers of strong repulsive forces; they repelled other particles and thus maintained their integrity. This was opposed by the view of atoms as having fixed sizes, composed of a material perfectly hard and impenetrable. Both theories had equal success in explaining the available evidence and both were long protected from discriminating test by virtue of the extreme smallness of the postulated atoms. True, the physical atoms would be larger than the point-atom but even its dimensions were well below the limits of both direct and indirect observation until well into the 20th century.

Now it seems the issue has been resolved in favor of the welcome compromise. Atoms do seem to have a size but that is in large part due to atomic forces that both control the sizes of the atomic components and determine their separation in space. Not only size, therefore, but shape is implied in the latest message from the laboratory. With shape began a whole new conception of matter. For it not only served as an essential clue to the behavior of ponderable substance, it raised profound questions about the connections between shape and function, about 'perfect shapes,' and about the nature of surfaces. These questions have not only a scientific significance but appear in different guises in many areas of human interest. To see that this is so, it may be best to turn from physics for a moment to the art of pedagogy.

II

There is a paradox that lies at the heart of all education. To turn the miraculous into the ordinary is profoundly destructive of that excited curiosity central to learning; yet the miraculous within the ordinary must be continually revealed to rekindle that excitement. At the great risk of making the marvelous and rich complexities of the world pedestrian in nature, education seeks to reveal the unexpected meanings and purpose behind the appearance. The word 'miraculous' is not meant to offend scientific sensibilities or to suggest connections with supernatural agencies. As Lord Kelvin perceived, there are in both the animate and inanimate world events and objects whose fundamental characters are utterly unknown and whose connections with our systems of scientific certainty are still extremely tenuous. These are the miracles referred to—not outside nature, but of nature. Indeed, so far removed are these from the ordinary miracles of religious traditions that the point is worth making for the contrast alone.

It was once believed that, in order to hear the voice of God, to receive visions of one's fate and messages from the Eternal—in short, to catch a glimpse of some high purpose to life—one had to go alone into the wilderness. There, in solitude and privation, the mind was swept clean and made receptive. Even today, mystical insight is often seen as impossible when the mind is teeming with the accumulations of private and social history. Being of devout character might help, but preoccupation with the mundane world is definitely a hindrance. No wonder, then, that these passively awaited experiences were and still are rare, unusual events, worthy of historical note within the religious traditions.

By contrast, the miracles of which I speak demand the prepared mind, the educated mind, a mind actively engaged in a process of wrestling to understand. How greatly is the human imagination magnified when aware of the patiently accumulated ideas and knowledge of others, it encounters a fossil fish or flint axe or meteoric iron. Education turns these meetings into possibilities for enriching experience precisely because it prepares the mind, not empties it.

The marvelous nature of these experiences is, ultimately, two-fold. Not only do we come to perceive the previously unguessed depths in the events and objects of the world, but at the same time we unavoidably reveal the subtleties and stratagems of the human mind as it struggles to uncover and understand this complexity. And the two are so necessarily interwoven that we're never sure which one we're doing at any time, which adds to the delightful frustration of it all.

Let me try and illustrate my meaning with a personal example. Many years ago, as a typically inattentive teenager, I sat, half-listening, half-dozing, as my physics teacher scrawled a long series of equations on the board. I can remember that they dealt with the motions of molecules of a gas confined to a fixed volume—like a sealed flask full of air. As such, though I didn't realize it then, the equations were both statistical and rigorous, attempting to impose order on what can only be described in understatement as a rather chaotic situation. In a naïve and unfocused manner, I tried to make a connection between those chalk symbols and the reality of the air-filled flask. Number, abstract quantity—could it really be used to describe the world? For that's what I wanted in my impatient youth; the world described. At first I was doubtful. Inside that flask billions of atoms were colliding with each other and the container's walls thousands of times a second at enormous speeds. I tried to imagine what it would be like to be such an atom, hurtling desperately out of control, endlessly suffering collision after collision. Could such an experience in any real way be described by the symbol P for pressure? And what of the molecules themselves, that both created and endured this pressure? If their speed and separation from one another could be represented by such a symbol, it seemed unlikely that they themselves would suffer the same abstraction, as the letter N for number. It was my first glimpse of the way physics loses the individual, as the macrocosm was reduced to the microcosm and beyond—to number.

It was only much later, encountering these same equations in adult life, indeed, being charged with teaching them to others, that I realized I had been given a glimpse of my first miracle. Groping in uncertain fashion with a realization of tremendous excitement and power, I found I could, in an imaginative leap, whirl chaotically through the molecule's wild dance and then translate that experience into the ordered world of numbers. There were, I sensed, two worlds, two kingdoms, contending for my attention. One was the mad, delightful kingdom of things, the rich world of given events. The other was the uniquely human kingdom of the mind, which seizes the other and compels it to order. Both could only be entered through the imagination; I could never fully know the true events of the molecules' frenzied path, and my equations therefore could never be a perfect representation. At best, they froze that chaos into a set of abstract symbols that the mind could creatively manipulate. The scientist, it seemed, is engaged in a translation of the events of nature into a human story we can act on. And in linking the two on the blackboard, my teacher had, perhaps unwittingly, revealed the dual nature of the miraculous to his students.

I spoke a moment ago of the loss of the individual in abstraction, as a feature of science. Here too shape has been a powerful guide to thought. Another of those great themes of physics that so puzzled Kelvin had been the conception of the world as either discrete or continuous. Indeed, the whole atomic hypothesis has been a commentary on this debate. In one sense, these dominant ideas can be expressed as the opposition between limits and connections. The individual is defined by its limits; boundary, size, form. Our common experience is always with individuals, with entities; the world appears given to us in discrete bits. Life, of course, depends upon identity, though it is strongly, necessarily connected to the rest of the world. We are, one the one hand, connected to the human world by speech and gesture and touch. On another, to the animals and plants through the great cycles of matter and energy that drive the organic world. Yet these connections, complex and large scale as they may be, are ultimately made between individuals—unique, separate. There are always barriers that oxygen, water—even love—must cross; there is a self. And to be a self there must be limits. In many religions, these limits are seen either as illusory to a mind swept clean of the mundane, or as challenges to faith in a divine One-ness. Through victory over the self, the individual experiences union with the unbounded. What follows is the record of one man's search for some understanding of such limits and the urge to transcend them, which is common to us all.

III

Like all things, this concern with limits has a history. In my case, it started with a problem with the edge of the universe. When I was a small boy, growing up in the suburbs of average American towns, I fell in love with astronomy. All at once I was dreaming around the solar system, landing on cratered moons, watching galaxies wheel and flame around me. I had it bad, the way it is when suddenly the Earth's too small and only the light year is a unit of sufficient scope. Being in my parents' minds, a suspiciously serious-minded youth, I didn't stop with the fantasy and frequently appalling pulp science fiction available in the local libraries. I haunted the science shelves for the big, luridly illustrated popular books on the subject. They took my incredulous young brain and set it spinning through a universe of incredible contrasts; the nightmare heat at the center of stars, stars that were flung through the absolute zero of space; great soundless explosions of supernovas; the crack of frozen methane of the stones of Neptune.

Finally, inevitably, as if tugged by the monstrous gravity of a neutron star, I came under the influence of cosmology. The beginnings of everything, absolutely everything, even time and distance; the impact of such ideas was overwhelming. Not that I clearly understood many of these concepts, of course. But I felt myself in the presence of great, important ideas that threw light on an unimaginable event, the instant of creation. When I began reading of these matters, the big debate was still raging between the Big Bang Theory and the Steady State Model. The former claimed that the universe began a finite time ago, at one moment, in a titanic explosion swelling the universe like a balloon, and at the same moment creating time and the very atoms of existence. Since at that time little could be guessed of the nature of the explosion itself, supporters of the theory were mostly working to find out if the swelling would keep on forever or if the whole thing would eventually slow down, stop, and collapse on itself. Adherents of the Steady State Model, on the other hand, were convinced that the universe was infinitely old and that it existed in a steady state of so many galaxies per cubic light year. Every once in a while, a single hydrogen atom would pop into existence somewhere, just balancing out the expansion's diminution of matter. Neither side could claim absolute victory, for some crucial data had still to come in. It was all tremendously exciting stuff for a young boy who had trouble peering out past the streetlights for a glimpse of Mars.

And since I had no real grasp of the evidence in this debate, I voted with my feelings and became a Steady Stater. It seemed somehow better to have an eternal, infinite universe than one with an edge. Or so I interpreted the Big Bang Model; even a balloon of space-time must have a boundary. Now this might seem like an arbitrary, if not perverse choice, revealing how little I had understood of the origins of time and space. Looking back, however, it now seems somehow tied up with the whole confusion of adolescence. It was a decision linked to the growing self-consciousness of youth; a self-consciousness that had become gropingly aware of boundaries in general. With experience comes wariness and the first glimpses of those light year chasms between minds that signal the real barriers in life. Very early I began to picture the social process as one of finding ways to bridge those gaps. There were words, of course, and sometimes these worked well. To my confusion and later delight, I eventually discovered what we all find—the gateways of the emotions, especially love and friendship. I was young, and those doors did not open easily, but I knew them.

Then, perhaps not coincidentally, came biology, and in one of those amazing transitions of childhood, I plunged from the crackling of interstellar radio sources to the frenetic chemistry of the cell. Though I never lost my interest in astronomy, my fascination with origins changed focus dramatically. I wanted to know the secret of life and followed the popularizers once again down into the physics and chemistry of cell components. Surely it was all a matter of the right chemical equations and laws of osmosis, diffusion, and heat flow? Life began, they hinted, as a series of unusual but hardly miraculous chemical processes in the sea, wrapped a protective membrane around itself, and turned into club mosses and dinosaurs. Nothing to it. Especially interesting was the cell membrane, that insulating wall between inside and outside. The boundary between one living thing and another fascinated me—there were pores, receptor sites, active transport, sensory cilia, phagocytosis to explore. Slowly I at last began to see the double-edged nature of those cell walls. From the physiologist Claude Bernard I learned to think of cellular life—and then of all life—as a war of inside versus outside, and that while inside won we lived. Life was indeed dependent on identity, on separateness. Yet so much of living seemed to be both acceptance of and rebellion against this truth, constantly seeking for ways to nullify the boundaries. It interacted closely with the inanimate world of rock, water, and air. It developed bizarre, intimate relationships with other organisms; so intimate that the dividing wall seemed to thin to the point of disappearance. It strove to change its form, bulging and distorting that cell wall from scaly fin to leaping reptile to soft down cracking from the egg. It acquired the habit of social living, sharing with and protecting others. And with us it achieved a new, perhaps ultimate reaching out—love, the pouring of one loneliness into that of another, dissolving as never before the essential rift.

It's plain to me now that I was in the grip of something bordering on an obsession. When out walking, I found I had an affinity for fences, especially those half-destroyed, long neglected fences that mark the edge of ploughed land, with forest behind. In the corners of paddocks, with trees leaning in and rusty wire holding the cultivated land back, I felt a strange, powerful agitation of the spirit. It symbolized for me, I believe now, the final breaking out of the natural world by our animal ancestors a million years ago, when they stepped for the last time from the thoughtless forest onto the furrowed land that led to the wheatened gold of still far distant cities. That too was a barrier crossed, and the old animate world still whispered to me as I sat leaning against a moss-covered corner post, the wires throwing thin shadows on the wind-swept highlands of my dreams.

And now? Now, by profession and interest, I'm lost in the depths of the atomic world. The empty space I assumed to exist between atoms has been shown to be filled with a sea of energy and virtual particles. There is not a single cubic centimeter of space anywhere in the universe where you could be truly alone. You would be riddled with the impact of particles so ephemeral that generations of them exist in a moment of thought. You would be bathed in the wash of energy that sweeps like a secret heartbeat throughout all space. Here, in the spaces between the atoms of my cells, the barriers are at last down, meaningless. Here, science seems to be saying to us, everything is really connected; particle to wave, knowledge to doing, today to tomorrow to yesterday. The barriers are our own conception, the result of the human way of thinking. Would that boy who first learned his physics as the loss of the individual be too surprised?

Yet of all this I am, at the last, still dubious. All can falter—knowledge, tomorrow, even love. And to compound my confusion, it now seems we Steady Staters were wrong, that the universe does have an edge. It separates everything from nothing. It is immeasurable in thought. I've still got this problem with the edge of the universe. True, I know now how hard we living things try to over-reach all the edges, all the limits. And I've walked enough fence lines, seeing the sun-whitened bones and broken, hollowed eggshells that gather in wind drifts there, to suspect that death leaves behind, in the end, only the barriers.

IV

It seems to me now that all my encounters with barriers, with membranes and edges, have been attempts to relieve the pain of a separation, that rift between inside and out. It may be there is a yearning at the center of all life to become one again; a yearning in direct opposition to the needs of life itself for identity. It represents, perhaps, the objection of matter to being caught up in the sweep of life. It is as though some vast cosmic Being, of incredible complexity and organizing power, longing to know itself in the eyes of another, has swept down on Earth and seized the silent, protesting elements for its own purposes. And while

91

grateful for a moment of consciousness and the warmth of the sun at mid-day, there remains this outage at the separation.

But in the end, I don't really believe in this conception of the origin of life. The image of a disembodied intelligence yearning through the universe for a home in matter is poetic but removed from the common miracles of which I spoke. I prefer the view that matter itself contains those 'dreadful powers' of which Hardy speaks—that somehow the secret of matter and the secret of life are the same. And now, as if following that curve of space-time that defines the universe, we round back toward the beginning. Think of the properties of matter and ask if somewhere in them is the secret of life. The earlier 20th century textbooks of physics, those familiar to Kelvin, paid more attention to them than is usual these days. Porosity, density, luster, conductivity, brittleness—can we find within such terms keys to the riddle of life and matter? Many scientists have hoped to do so, to find the answers to cellular life in the electrical, mechanical, and chemical attributes of matter. And of course, to some extent they were, and are, right. But where in this great intellectual effort is the property that will explain the human concern with limits?

The biochemists have argued that the complex and infinitely variable shapes of large molecules such as DNA can serve as templates for the information necessary for life. In the same way, many of the physical and chemical properties of matter are linked to shape—porosity and malleability are examples. Enzyme activity also seems clearly linked to molecular shape, which thus determines the metabolism of life.

In my own case, shape also provides a metaphor of great power for pondering the nature of the human world. Two expressions in everyday use can illustrate this; the shape of a life and the influences which have shaped the future. What can these mean? Part of the answer is that shape defines and limits possibilities; it allows distinctions to be made. In this sense, a life can have a shape in the possibilities that are realized and in the dominant projections of the self into the moment and the future. A life without such 'shape' takes the form of its surrounds, like water in a bowl, and shows a limited possibility of freezing into coherent personality.

Shape also allows points of attachment and safe harbor. The shape of a life can provide unique anchors for joy, pain, envy, until we bristle with attached symbionts like antigens surrounding a bacterium. Perhaps too there are shaped receptor sites in the mind for certain thoughts or ideas, which we therefore find so right as to be unquestionable. Removing them would be literally an uprooting, and new ideas rarely seem to be quite the right fit. It would, in that sense, be somehow fitting if shape was to be found to be a key to understanding human personality.

The other half of shape, of course, is nothingness—the space inside the cup which holds the water; the slot into which the bolt is thrown. With shape must come the existence of an inside and an outside. And as you run your fingertips gently over the features of a loved face, there is the consciousness that this is a surface, the outside of one forever fixed within this form, accessible only through those uniquely human gifts of love and friendship. If to possess these, it was necessary that barriers be raised in the name of life, then the bargain was well struck. In our struggle with limits, in our efforts to understand and overcome them, we reveal the bittersweet nature of our human selves.

Solubility

"...to remain dissolved, is both the obligation and the privilege of all substances that are destined (I was about to say 'wish') to change.

Primo Levi

I

I've always thought it a shame and a sign of lack of foresight on the part of evolution that we can't drink seawater. Our cells picked up the salt and lime habit a long time ago, due to our origins in the early oceans, and as a result our blood needs to have a salt concentration close to that of seawater. Our sweat is salty, as are our tears. I have this picture in my mind of some group of very early humans, long nurtured in some isolated inland area of Africa, coming to terms with life as a thinking being. They have real concerns with food and water. And one day, wandering along a newly discovered, nearly dry riverbed, they get their first glimpse of the ocean. Whatever else they may be thinking about it at that moment, one thing it seems to me must occur to all of them rather soon; "Boys, our water problems are over!" Alas, not so; their disappointment must have been as sharp as their wits allowed back then.

All that water, and all that salt; we need them both, but unfortunately not together. As a science teacher, talking with students about this misfortune, I used to comment apropos of nothing at all that I did think evolution got it wrong there. But it also occurred to me that maybe chemistry could come in for its share of the blame. If salt wasn't able to dissolve in water, then the seas might have been able to begin working on other lines right from the start. Fresh water oceans; maybe on some other planet they surge under the influence of strange moons and harbor life of a different chemistry, forming different habits.

But salt does dissolve, along with a great multitude of other substances; solids, liquids, and gases. Water is a powerful solvent, one of the best there is, and therefore, despite my petulant annoyance, the perfect medium for life. Life needs to have things happen, and happen under its control. And, on this planet anyway, the best place for that to happen is in solution, where diverse materials can be brought together and allowed to interact. What after all is a cell but a drop of water with lots of intricate and diverse components in dynamic interaction, wrapped in a waterproof membrane?

II

Solubility—a term used to describe, and sometimes measure, the extent to which one substance, termed the solute, will dissolve in another, the solvent. It may seem that we have only used one word to define another without any gain in understanding. Dissolve itself has two possible physical meanings. In the first, the solute is reduced to molecular size but retains its chemical identity. An example is sugar. In the second, the solute is more fully disassembled, reduced to component parts. An example is salt. In the first case, we might agree that there has been no loss of identity, only a greater or lesser degree of dispersion; our lump of sugar now sweetens our large glass of lemonade. In more molecular terms, our lump of sugar was composed of a multitude of sucrose molecules all heaped together but without chemical bonds uniting them; dissolving merely separates them one from another, granting a freedom but not a change in structure. In the case of salt, it does appear that there has been a true change in identity. Table salt, as it comes from the shaker, is a crystalline solid composed of sodium and chloride ions locked in regular array. Once placed in water, the lattice dissociates, freeing the ions to behave independently. And in this case, the freedom of the ions allows the solution to show behaviors that the water alone did not possess.

Indeed, this change of behavior is at the very heart of the powerful influence of solubility on the chemistry of life and matter. A solvent like water with a dissolved solute is now something that it was not before. It has been altered by its solutes. It may now, for example, conduct electricity. It may emit light or heat. It may attract pure water to itself. And indeed prove inimical to the needs of life. Loss of identity of the solute permits the formation of something new, creating possibilities, allowing, as Primo Levi tells us, change.

Of course, in all this we must not fail to consider the question of scale. In ordinary usage, we assume a small amount of solute to be added to a large amount of solvent, as with our lump of sugar or grains of salt. We can picture such disparities as large as we like, leading to nearly infinite dilution and the new properties of the solution as negligible. In a tangible sense, this is now a real, practical matter as we try to determine how many bucketfuls of smoke and ash we can dissolve in the huge reservoirs of our atmosphere and oceans before the effects become of significance. Some scientists urge that the only safe amount is zero; they are the ones most disturbed by dissolving.

On another level is the practice of homeopathy, with its extremely minute amounts of solute given in the effort to heal. This operates on the idea that minute amount of the substance that causes the symptoms of a disease can be used to cure that disease; the concept of 'like cures like.' The truth of this claim is not the concern of this moment. But it is suggestive of a similar concept in chemistry that 'like dissolves like.' This is of such importance to solubility that it needs further attention.

For the student, as for the metaphysician, the question becomes—like in what manner? Salt dissolves in water; in what ways are these two alike? At first glance they appear almost diametrically opposite. Liquid versus solid. Molecule versus ionic crystal lattice. Water is composed of hydrogen and oxygen, two gases, both in the form of atoms. Salt is a metal and a gas, both in the form of their respective ions. In our case, the likeness is found at the level of electric charge. Water molecules are so constructed by their bonding forces as to have a positive and a negative end. We say they are polar. Salt, when placed in water, finds its lattice attacked by these polar molecules, separating as a result into positively charged sodium ions and negatively charged chloride ion. These then disperse throughout the water medium. In contrast, oils, possessing no such charge are unlike and thus float to the top.

III

Like dissolves like. Comparisons with society and the assimilation of the foreign are obvious. In education, the analogy is just as intriguing. I like to think of the mind as a solvent and an idea as a solute. How much more easily the familiar, the expected, the only slightly different is taken in, its influence perhaps small but present. A bit more salt or a different salt has little effect on the seasoning. The challenge in education, it seems to me, is to get the unlike, the foreign, to dissolve. This is, of course, the main task of pedagogy. There are two possible approaches.

One, make the unlike into like. By disguise, by altering it into something familiar. Show that it is really just the same as something they already know. Two, change the nature of the solvent. From polar to non-polar, from water to oil.

The first of these two options has been the usual approach, and of course it has met with mixed success. This has been the role of analogy, of models, and perhaps most powerfully of metaphor. In the teaching of science, at any rate, great attention has been paid to using such tools as bridges, linking like and unlike. Think of light as if it were a water wave, we tell them. Picture your elbow as if it were a child's seesaw. Some of these bridges appear so helpful they have persisted in the textbooks for generations. But the teachers' experience suggests that it is not enough to present a ready-made bridge to the student. What makes learning more truly a homogeneous solution is for the student to construct the bridge for themselves, to actively turn unlike into like.

The second approach is interesting to explore. Imagine an intelligent solvent, capable of recognizing the nature of the solute and altering its own chemistry accordingly. Of course, there is now the risk that, upon changing its chemistry, some if not all the previously dissolved items will come out of solution and precipitate to the bottom; a circumstance that must be avoided at all costs. I have often contemplated the advantages of such a mind and tried to imagine how, as a teacher, I might encourage the creation of such a mental solvent in my students.

Even if that were possible, the story is not yet over. We know from life as well as from chemistry that how much of a solute will dissolve depends crucially on several factors, such as temperature and pH of the solvent, and any pressures acting. For example, oxygen dissolves better in cold water than warm. So the teacher's task is to create those conditions under which the greatest amount of new knowledge can dissolve; to me, this is the art of pedagogy. In education, those conditions are numerous and ill understood. Learning styles, social setting, genetic variability, curriculum structure, time available; all of these and many more make the teacher into artist and craftsperson and hard-won empiricist.

I spoke deliberately above of the mind as a solvent, avoiding the term brain. I did this for two reasons. If the idea is to dissolve like into like and if what is to be dissolved is a concept or item of knowledge, then such an immaterial solute can only reasonably be expected to dissolve into an equally immaterial solvent. The brain may be the thought of as the container in which the solvent mind is found. Secondly, I believe that the way to think of a mind that is capable of changing its structure to match any given solute is not changing brain states but changing character. The ability to recognize and assimilate and indeed welcome the foreign is a matter of character and ethos.

My first high school teaching job was at a steel mill suburb of Wollongong, New South Wales. Many of my students were the children of recently arrived migrants from Eastern Europe. My teacher training had paid no attention to the problem of teaching science to students for whom English was a second, rudimentary language. In effect, my problem was getting science words to dissolve in an unlike solvent. Turning unlike into like. It was based pretty heavily on nouns at first. I might hold up a test tube and give its name; they would chorus it back to me, and then I would ask for its name in their language. At first there would be mocking laughter from those of other language groups. But gradually the laughter turned to silence and then evolved into a shared amusement. The acquisition of a shared language, even of commonplace or unusual items of laboratory equipment and procedures, helped turned unlike into like.

During lunchtime, the boys would spend their time aggressively re-enacting the national and ethnic discords of their fathers, asserting the predominance of Croatia over Serbia or Yugoslavia. The boys from Poland came in for their share of the mutual hostility, fighting battles that no longer served any purpose. Eventually, though perhaps it might take a generation, their differences would be dissolved in the commonality of thinking of themselves as Australians. But in the classroom, the science classroom at least, the atmosphere was different. At that time, there were only two places in the school where students had to work in groups; the science lab and the sports field. It's the same the world over, I think; those who either have a certain drive to succeed or have an innate gift for something, gravitate to those with whom they can work productively. I've seen it happen in every class; when allowed to choose their groups the able are soon working together, regardless of age or ethnicity or race. It's even been said to me that friendships get in the way. Perhaps in terms of our metaphor we could say that here, like seeks out like.

IV

Two of the central questions in learning are: how much has been learned, and how much can be learned. The answer to the first is the sort of thing we seek to determine with the inevitable end of term exam. If the mind is a solvent, how much solute has it dissolved is one part of that answer. The other part is, out of all that has been dissolved, how much has the student been able to precipitate out of solution for presentation to the exam markers?

To answer the second question, what we are always asking ourselves as teachers is, what are the best conditions for learning to take place? How can we increase the amount of solute that actually enters into solution? In the latter case, we already know a great deal about how to do this.

For example, we can grind the solute down to smaller and smaller particles before adding it to the solvent. This increases the surface area of the particles so more is in contact with the molecules of solvent, hastening the process of dissolution. In science education it has become commonplace that we reduce the amount of material to be learned into smaller units first. We don't talk about solubility for example until we have introduced the idea of what a solute is. Later, we put the pieces together in a larger and larger picture, gradually increasing the amount of new information now safely in solution.

Or we add the solute and stir. Or shake; either will usually do, though preferences are well known. The action of stirring repeatedly puts fresh particles in contact with the solvent, again quickening the desired process. In the classroom, such stirring is equivalent to bringing one fresh example of a process after another to the attention of the student in order, by multiplying examples, to encourage the entry of the idea into the correct location in the mind.

Another factor that affects how much can be learned is how much has been learned already. Here we are on more paradoxical ground. In solutions, the more that has been dissolved, the less you can add, of course, until you reach saturation and no more will enter into solution. In the science lab, things are more complicated. On one hand, we need to worry about information overload, offering too much too quickly for the mind to absorb. Having that in mind, we also recognize that the more we know about something, the more we can know because there are more places for the new information to hook onto. There are more spaces that are ready to recognize the new as like something known already. Once the concept of solubility has taken hold, one might say, it is easier for the student to move onto the laws governing its applicability in diverse types of solvents or in combinations with other solutes.

Perhaps the factor that most quickly comes to mind that strongly affects the amount of solute that can be dissolved is the temperature of the solvent. But here again, things are not as straightforward as they might seem.

For example, two easily dissolved substances such as salt and sugar differ greatly in their solubility in water of different temperatures. Both follow the general rule for solid solutes, that as the temperature of the water increases, the amount that dissolves increases as well. But the values are quite different. For sucrose, the amount that dissolves in water of near freezing, around 0°C, is 181.9 grams in every 100 mL of water. At 100°C, this increases to 476 grams per 100 mL. But salt hardly changes at all, staying pretty constant between 35.65 and 38.99 grams per 100 mL across that temperature range.

But for gases, the basic rules change. Gases tend to dissolve better the colder the water. Oxygen, for example, shows a decrease of over 2.2 times in the amount that can dissolve as the water temperature rises from 0 to 40°C. Hence, there is more oxygen available to fish that live in cold oceans than in warm, accounting in part for the huge but dwindling fisheries of the northern seas. The explanation here has to do with the kinetic energy of the water molecules. Cold water is cold because the molecules are moving slower, therefore having more opportunity to meet and interact with the faster moving gas molecules, again speeding up the process. Here the teacher wants a warm mind but one under deliberate control, taking its time to make sure all its interactions with the new ideas have time to form the links that ensure dissolving. Like meets like but needs time to recognize that it is like.

V

Solubility is a property of matter of immense importance to the chemist and industrialist. Its investigation at the molecular and atomic level has been intense and is ongoing. In its biological aspects, it is a chief determinant of the possibility of cellular life, for without the multiple solutes interacting in a drop of water, the chemical reactions that are indeed what we think of as life could not take place. Bringing like and unlike together, allowing exchange and combination and change, the conditions for transformation from inorganic to organic are realized.

Exchange, combination, and change. These are the means by which matter is made to speak. The stones are not mute, the winds have voices that sing of arrival and departure, of chaos and calm. By deep and difficult labor, the human ear has come to know this singing. It has come to us through close attention, through the millennia of our trials and errors with this bedrock of our existence.

It is this singing, these voices that the teachers of science want the students to hear. It is not enough to know the tables of solubility, the molecular causes of dissolution or precipitation. There must be a moment, an experience, which makes matter's voice stir the mind and spirit to wonder.

High school science teachers can get asked to do things that involve them in aspects of school life that are normally rather remote from their own classrooms. Some years ago, I was teaching in a small Catholic school in Tasmania which had a large number of students from a middle European background. The school decided to put on a year 8 play based on a Balkan fairy tale. Roles were allocated and rehearsals begun when I was approached by the drama teacher. Could I arrange for the fairy godmother to change water into gold? After being convinced she was serious and realizing that both my expertise and my entire curriculum area was being challenged by the arts faculty, I replied, "Sure, why not?" Having gained my acceptance of this minor problem, she went on to tell me that we were talking about enough water to fill a fish tank, and "it had to be done right," by which she meant clearly visible right up to the back row and right on time, without smoke or smell or danger to the cast, crew, or audience.

Now this kind of thing can be done but it was going to take some work. I had only a faint memory of the chemicals used, and back in those days, there was no internet to search. Phone calls were made and chemical supply houses contacted. Two of the ingredients needed were easy to obtain and relatively inexpensive; glacial acetic acid and sodium thiosulfate. Both are common industrially, and most high school science labs have some on the shelf. But not in the quantities I needed for a fish tank size result. But the third was quite unusual and rather more expensive; sodium arsenite is used as a pesticide and dyeing agent. But it is also listed as a hazardous substance and has strict safety precautions associated with its use. This last piece of information I kept to myself, relying on the fact that it would be in solution and, in theory, no one should be exposed to it directly. I had to spend some time negotiating with the Principal for the money to purchase the amount of this I needed and then ensure no one saw it arrive at the school covered in hazardous chemical warnings.

I didn't have much of these chemicals to play around with, so testing it out was a little less than rigorous. I ended up making two solutions; solution A was composed of 5 liters of water, 550 mL of glacial acetic acid, and 100 grams of sodium arsenite. When combined into a solution, it was clear as water. This was placed in the fish tank. Solution B was only 1 liter of water, with 300 grams of sodium thiosulfate mixed in. It too was clear but it took some doing to get all that solute dissolved in that little water. Ideally, both solutions should have the same volume, but the fairy godmother had to lift up and pour Solution B, and 1 liter was about all she could handle, so I made it more concentrated to compensate. I placed it in a suitably decorated Erlenmeyer flask, made to look kind of medieval, I suppose. And there was not enough of either to allow for a rehearsal complete with the desired result, so the actors had to pretend it was happening in front of their eyes. The drama teacher was unhappy with this infraction of the rules of rehearsing, but I told her if she used it up before the big night, that was her problem. I admit, though, I was getting increasingly nervous about all this. Chemistry is an exact science until you start to play around with things like you do in a fairy tale, and I was not totally at ease about the whole thing. There was no way, for example, to work out what might be the result when solution A, spending an hour under hot studio lights, gained a few degrees while solution B stayed cool as a cucumber behind the throne.

The big night finally arrives, and the thing gets underway. I had been told to stand off stage and out of sight, but I could see that the front row of the school hall was filling with family and relatives of the starring princess. Her paternal grandfather, who we had all met before at other school functions, was sitting front row center. As the play develops, the princess is kidnapped by an evil knight who holds her to ransom, to be saved by the handsome prince. But just as he arrives after fighting his way through two or three incredible feats of arms, he finds his princess turned to stone by a sorcerer on the side of the wicked. There is only one way to break the spell and defeat the forces of evil. The good fairy godmother, who has been assisting the prince and princess all along, must turn water into gold. The moment is coming, and I notice that the grandfather is getting more and more involved in the horrible fate his granddaughter has found herself in. He is on the edge of his seat and his eyes are burning. *God,* I think, *if this doesn't come off we are all in trouble.* I glance back at the drama teacher and find she is looking at me with that look that tells me that trouble would be coming from other directions as well.

At the bidding of the fairy godmother, the prince goes to the throne and retrieves solution B. He holds it up to her and she gives it a blessing. I didn't remember that in the plot but I felt like blessing it as well. Finally, after holding it dramatically aloft for a few seconds, she slowly pours it into solution A, pronouncing some arcane spell as she does so. Well, it wasn't all that arcane; I had suggested earlier that the best thing to say was $NaASO2$, the formula for sodium arsenite; when pronounced as a single word it was suitably magical. Now what I hadn't told anyone was that the reaction of these two is not instantaneous; it can take up to 30 seconds. I had the best of reasons for not telling anyone this because I didn't have a clue myself how long it was going to take and I was hoping for the best. For about a lifetime there wasn't a sound in the hall, from audience or cast or crew. Maybe, if you can hear someone holding their breath, you could have heard from me. Then just as I felt the drama teacher take a step in my direction, and the grandfather seemed about to leap from his chair, the gleam of gold began within the fish tank and slowly and calmly and majestically spread from top to bottom. Under the stage lights, it gleamed and sparkled and shone; it was, I thought then, the most beautiful thing I had ever seen. There was a gasp from the audience, and suddenly the grandfather jumped to his feet and shouted, "Saved! By the powers of heaven, saved!" He stood with tears running down his face as the prince took his awakening love by the hand and led her to the throne, where she sat in royal pomp and dignity.

"So, that's what you call chemistry, is it?" said a voice from behind. I turned to find the drama teacher standing with a frown on her face but a light in her eyes.

"Yes, that's it, alright. Any more little problems like that, just come to me." But it was not quite over yet, for me at any rate. I had to find a way of safely removing that toxic solution before someone decided to put their hands in it and retrieve some of the 'gold.' I hastily flung the prince's cloak over the tank and got one of the older stagehands to help me carry it out to the science lab. Like I said, the science teacher gets all kinds of unusual requests, but this was the only time I have been asked to become an alchemist.

Bibliography

Bizzell, P. and Herzberg, B. (2000). *The Rhetorical Tradition*. Bedford/St. Martins, U.K.

Bronowski, J. (1978). *Magic, Science and Civilization*. Columbia University Press, New York.

Eiseley, L. (1962). *Francis Bacon and the Modern Dilemma*. University of Nebraska Press, U.S.A.

Eiseley, L. (1972). *Notes of an Alchemist*. Charles Scribners, New York.

Eiseley, L. (1959). *The Immense Journey*. Vintage Books, New York.

Huxley, T. H. (1902). *Introductory*. London: Macmillan.

Huxley, T. H. (1868). *On a Piece of Chalk*. Oriole Editions, New York.

Levi, P. (2010). *The Periodic Table*. Penguin, U.K.

Medawar, P. B. (1982). *Pluto's Republic*. Oxford University Press, Oxford.

Monod, J. (1972). *Chance and Necessity*. William Collins, Great Britain.

Mumford, L. (1952). *Art and Technics*. Columbia University Press, New York.
Robinson, A. (2006). *The Last Man Who Knew Everything*. Pi Press, U.S.A.

Santayana, G. (1995). *The Birth of Reason and Other Essays*. Columbia University Press, New York.

Stevens, W. (2015). *The Collected Poems of Wallace Stevens*. Vintage Books, New York.